NAVIGATE YOUR CAREER TRANSITION

STRATEGIES FOR NURSE LEADERS

Deborah A. Yancer, MS, RN

Julie Klausen Moe, MSN, RN, *Editors*

 American Hospital Publishing, Inc.,
An American Hospital Association company
Chicago

This publication is designed to provide accurate and authoritative information in regard to the subject matter covered. It is sold with the understanding that neither the authors nor the publisher is engaged in rendering legal, accounting, or other professional service. If legal advice or other expert assistance is required, the services of a competent professional person should be sought.

The views expressed in this publication are strictly those of the authors and do not necessarily represent official positions of the American Hospital Association.

Library of Congress Cataloging-in-Publication Data

Navigate your career transition : strategies for nurse leaders /
   edited by Deborah Yancer and Julie Klausen Moe.
      p.   cm.
   Includes bibliographical references.
   ISBN 1-55648-182-9
   1. Nursing services—Administration—Vocational guidance.
2. Career changes. I. Yancer, Deborah A. II. Moe, Julie Klausen.
   [DNLM: 1. Nursing, Supervisory. 2. Job Application.
3. Employment. 4. Adaptation, Psychological. WY 29 N325 1997]
RT89.N39 1997
610.73′06′9—dc21
DNLM/DLC
for Library of Congress   96-44580
                                                  CIP

Catalog no. 088176

©1997 by American Hospital Publishing, Inc.,
an American Hospital Association company

Printed in the USA

ꓮꓧꓮ is a service mark of the American Hospital Association used under license by American Hospital Publishing, Inc.

Text set in Palacio

American Hospital Publishing, Inc.
737 North Michigan Avenue
Chicago, Illinois 60611

Contents

About the Editors

Deborah A. Yancer, MS, RN, CNAA, is vice-president, patient services, and chief nursing officer, Saint Thomas Hospital, Nashville, TN. She has 21 years of progressive experience in hospital operations, 16 years at the executive level and 5 years in staff and management roles. Yancer served as chief operating officer with Alegent Health–Bergan Mercy Medical Center in Omaha, NE. Yancer has also provided consultation to organizations and given conference presentations on a variety of topics, including changing health care trends, career transitions, shared governance, and empowerment models. She is an active member of the American Organization of Nurse Executives and has held office at the state and national levels. Yancer is an experienced author with several articles and abstracts in print and a second book in the final stages of development. She holds an MS degree in nursing from the University of Kansas and a BS degree in nursing from Andrews University, Berrien Springs, MI. She is certified by the American Nursing Association in nursing administration, advanced.

Julie Klausen Moe, RN, MSN, is manager for special projects for Alegent Health–Bergan Mercy Medical Center in Omaha, NE. In this position she facilitates the development of new programs, systems, and services and serves as an internal consultant for major organizational change efforts. She conducts issue research and analysis, contributes extensive project support, and provides professional and technical writing for the organization. Moe also consults with other health care organizations in the areas of nursing administration, project assistance, and systems development. Moe has published a number of articles about nursing and management in professional health care journals. Additionally, she has contributed to several health care books, including ones on nursing care planning and nursing shared governance. Moe received a Master of Science in Nursing Administration at the University of Texas Medical Branch at Galveston, Galveston, TX.

About the Contributors

JoAnne Kennebeck, JD, RN, has held various administrative and executive positions in hospitals and health care associations throughout the Midwest. She is a graduate of Drake University Law School.

Katherine W. Vestal, PhD, RN, is vice-president and managing director of health care consulting for the Hay Group, Dallas, leading a highly respected, fully integrated national practice that assists numerous clients with a wide range of organizational and management issues. Vestal has been featured at a number of national and international health care conferences, written numerous articles for professional journals, and published several books on health care topics. Before joining the Hay Group, she was a partner at Ernst & Young. Prior to that, she held several executive positions in large teaching hospitals and served as a university professor. She holds a BSN from Texas Christian University, an MS from Texas Women's University, and a PhD from Texas A&M University. She is a member of the American College of Health Care Executives, a Johnson & Johnson Fellow of the Wharton School of Finance, and a Fellow in the American Academy of Nursing.

Foreword

The up-and-coming health professional now has to negotiate each career move. Formerly, there was a career path one could follow, but this path is no longer evident. Today, jobs come and go, new opportunities emerge in unexpected ways, and traditional career path jobs aren't what they used to be. The circumstances require a new approach to making career transitions. Deborah Yancer, Julie Klausen Moe, JoAnne Kennebeck, and Katherine Vestal have each in their own way studied the various aspects of this approach, and in this book they present their findings. Even the title, *Navigate Your Career Transition*, encapsulates the new mind-set health care professionals must develop to move successfully away from the old approach to developing one's career, toward the new one.

Sometimes, new opportunities for nurse leaders just seem to "happen" if they go with the flow. Other times, nurse leaders search for months to find these opportunities. In either case, the key ingredients to successful career development stay virtually the same. One must believe in his or her own capabilities; must be competent in clinical, financial, and organizational practices; must work continuously on relationships and networking; and must never assume anything. In these changing times, expectations shift rapidly and tensions abound. Beyond competence, the nurse leader who is adaptable and well connected has more opportunities than those who seek to shape the world in the image of their preestablished view of the health care system. In the midst of change, personal and professional values and a view of future potentials for improving health care delivery are more critical than knowledge of past practices.

There is both an art and a science to making successful career transitions. During the job search, the personal impact and, often, the pain of loss may get in the way of recognizing and utilizing one's own talents. This book provides an effective intervention. Learning how to go about a career transition and acting on the realities of a job search are strategies that can be employed to move from the past to the future. The key point to remember in using this excellent book is that every career transition starts with two essentials: a need to succeed and a purpose. Belief in oneself and one's capabilities fuels the process. Knowing how to make a career transition is the vehicle to take you there.

Marjorie Beyers, PhD, RN, Executive Director,
American Organization of Nurse Executives

Preface

The world of work has changed dramatically in the past decade. Mergers and acquisitions, leveraged buyouts, reorganizations, and consolidations have invaded and nearly taken over the vocabulary of today's business. The health care industry is no exception. Downsizing, redesigning, and repositioning are common as health care organizations attempt to redefine their business and systems, reduce costs, and remain competitive. Changes in health care reimbursement are causing substantial shifts in patient activity and service utilization. Mergers and acquisitions are on the rise, with 650 reported in process during 1994.* Further, hospital closures have averaged more than 60 for the past 4 years and are expected to increase in number in the coming years.**

These changes have had a tremendous impact on the health care institution's hierarchy. Management positions are being eliminated, and the responsibilities of the remaining managers greatly altered. The revolution in the structure of the health care industry will guarantee that we will work in many different jobs and most likely several different organizations during our careers. Given the present volatile nature of the health care industry, it is difficult, almost impossible, for organizations to make or keep promises about employment security. Because we no longer can rely on our employer for job security, we must become responsible for our own career security.

Purpose of This Book

This book responds to the need for a concise and relevant tool to support career transitions for health care managers and executives. Although

*Lutz, S. (1994) Let's make a deal: healthcare mergers, acquisitions take place at dizzying pace. *Modern Healthcare* (Dec. 19–26), p. 47.
** Greene, J. (1992) Hospitals now merge rather than close. *Modern Healthcare* (Jul. 6) , pp. 20–21.

numerous books are available on various aspects of general job searching, this book specifically addresses the changes occurring in health care and how nurse leaders can be prepared to successfully face a career transition.

Audience for This Book

Navigate Your Career Transition was developed for nurses in management and executive practice. These are the nurses most frequently affected by mergers, acquisitions, and work redesign efforts. Many are unprepared to either apply for positions within their current organization or pursue other opportunities. This book serves as a guide for nurse leaders to attain and maintain search readiness when their positions seem secure, as well as to help them cope effectively with job loss and launch a successful job search.

Overview

Navigate Your Career Transition is organized into five chapters. Chapter 1, "Preparing for an Unexpected Career Transition," discusses the chaotic nature of the health care industry and the necessity for employees to take responsibility for ensuring their employment security. It includes methods for assessing an organization for potential warning signs of transition and steps that nurse executives can take to remain search ready at all times. Chapter 2, "Coping with Job Loss," focuses on the emotional issues facing those who are unemployed. It offers suggestions on how to manage the exit from a position, cope with the inevitable emotional responses that will follow, and improve negative attitudes in order to move forward with a productive job search. Chapter 3, "Organizing and Managing the Job Search," presents the specific steps necessary to begin and sustain a successful job search. Included are methods to determine personal career needs, assess the industry, formulate a plan to get the job, develop the tools for the job search, and market yourself effectively. Chapter 4, "Achieving and Documenting Employment Agreements," illustrates how to secure the terms and conditions of employment you want and how to ensure that these agreements are in a legally enforceable form. Formal written employment contracts, severance agreements, offer and acceptance letters, and letters of agreement are explained, as are strategies for principled negotiations. The first four chapters of the book include "Common Questions and Answers," reviewing material covered in the chapter. Finally, Chapter 5, "Managing the Trauma of Involuntary

Termination: A Case Study," presents an actual example of a nurse executive experiencing involuntary and unexpected job loss. Excerpts from her journal are provided as a record of her thoughts and feelings, followed by author commentary applying the principles described throughout this book.

Currents

Currents pull us,
tides, crosswinds.
We come out of an eddy
in a stream, into a
narrow place,
a curve where
water has a
power we must move with.

The river has its strength,
the pull of stream downhill
in white water, around
a bend, the power of
the seas and oceans, too,
the tides.

And we have choices still
in how we are
within that flow,
as if reedlike we float
so that the current pours
within and through us,
or else in grasping not to go
to some new place,
we lodge crosswise
and broken against rocks,
safely unmoving and
yet crushed by force
of water pushing against us.

We have a choice,
not of the current,
but of the way
we turn ourselves
within its strength.

We cannot foil the tides
but we can learn the timing
and the grace of turning
so that force of water
gives us strength,
and helps us on our way
to some new place we
didn't mean to go,
yet where we can arrive
in safety, with exhilaration,
gratitude, relief,
still whole and even more ourselves
for having found a way to be
in partnership with currents
we had not anticipated.

—Judy Brown
printed with permission

Chapter 1

Preparing for an Unexpected Career Transition

Deborah A. Yancer, MS, RN

N urse leaders are experiencing career transitions with growing frequency. This trend is partly due to the rapid changes occurring in
health care. How do we make sense of the changes and position ourselves for success? In the poem at the front of this book, Judy Brown
paints a picture of learning to move in partnership with the currents of
a river. So must we, on our career path, learn to partner with unanticipated changes, learn the timing and the grace of turning so that the force
of changes gives us strength and helps us on our way to some new place
we did not mean to go. Understanding the change in employment
dynamics nationwide is the first step toward building for ourselves a
career lifeline, if you will, a source of preparedness and tools to draw
upon during times of tumultuous change to assure our safe journey
through career transitions.

This chapter discusses today's changing dynamics of employment
in general and of employment of nurse executives and nurse managers
in particular. It also outlines the elements essential to developing a "career
lifeline," a survival strategy for making career transitions.

Changing Employment Dynamics

Although we all would like to believe that our jobs are important and
will always be needed, this is simply not the case. As society continues
to change and reshape itself from an industrial society to an information society, jobs also are being reshaped.[1] And because most new jobs
are in the service arena, even industries such as health care are being
reshaped.[2] Whether it is called "reengineering," "work redesign," or
"patient-focused care," the process of redefining work that is occurring
right now in health care centers around the movement from functional,
or discipline-specific, work toward cross-functional, or shared, work.
Most new designs share the common goal of integrating work and workers

across organizations for the purposes of improving efficiency and reducing cost.

As organizations seek ways to reduce their expenses, payroll is a common target. The effect of layoffs and employment reductions in American industries is staggering. "One family in ten has someone out of work. One half of all workers know someone who has lost a job. One third expect someone in their families to be laid off in the next twelve months." It is no wonder, then, that the number one fear of middle-class Americans is unemployment.[3]

Hand in hand with this scenario is the growing trend toward using temporary or outsourced staffing. This measure allows employers to flex the size of their workforce without sustaining the burden of ongoing benefit expenses or undergoing the trauma of staff reductions. Temporary workers can be added or canceled as needed, to respond to business needs. This trend reflects the growing shift away from thinking of work as a job toward viewing it as work to be done.

The Movement toward Employees Assuming Responsibility for Their Own Employability

In the United States, there is a strong movement afoot in both business and the government to redefine the concept of job security. This redefinition does not eliminate job security but, rather, presents it in a new form called *employment security,* or even better, *employability.* Instead of being assigned a specific job, employees will have skills and benefits that are portable. These transformations represent more than a small change in thinking and place responsibility for employment squarely with the employee.[4] In fact, employers are encouraging workers to view themselves as self-employed — working under contract, as it were, for various employers throughout their career. Rosabeth Moss Kanter suggests that employers guarantee the employability of their workers by providing them with opportunities to continually update their skills. Thus, the guarantee of employability replaces the previous commitment to guarantee employment.[5,6]

The shift in responsibility for employment from employer to employee underscores the fact that it is increasingly uncommon for workers to remain in the same job or company throughout their careers. In fact, most workers will change careers three to four times in their lifetime and will have as many as 13 different jobs.[7]

Workers secure in their ability to acquire employment are those who plan proactively, watch the job market, and acquire marketable skills. Employment security is something they create for themselves by applying the necessary resources, intellectual and educational, to the task of obtaining employment. Such workers do not look to employers to provide jobs but, rather, demonstrate their value to employers to acquire work.[8,9] In that way, employers shift from being caretakers to being customers. Thus, a worker's future success will depend on his or her ability to constantly update and create the right mix of knowledge and skills, and to market his or her value.[10] Tom Peters sums it up well: "The only security in the world where job security is gone is that your skills are better and your network richer at the end of this year than they were at the beginning."[11]

The Emergence of New Organizational Forms

Today, new organizational forms are emerging that can be changed as needed to respond to the changing needs of business. A. Baber and L. Waymon compare these new organizational forms to colored chips in a kaleidoscope, which can be figured and reconfigured into temporary patterns.[12] Their description is particularly insightful. Historically, organizational forms have been predominantly of the hierarchical type, and when changes occurred, they did so slowly and seemed to be similar in design to previous structures. However, future organizations, especially those that are most capable of responding to frequent changes, will have more flexible designs. Figure 1-1 contrasts traditional and fully coordinated organizations and their needs for structure and supervision.

As organizations redesign, one clear action in common across industries has been the reduction of management positions. Partly because of the nature of the work in an information society and partly due to the rapidity of change, decision making and action must be placed close to the customer. Thus, the worker is being given more autonomy to act, and there is less need for hierarchy. The minimization of organizational hierarchy is resulting in serious reductions in the management workforce. In hospitals, management positions have been reduced significantly, in many cases by 50 percent. A target used by one health care consulting firm is to reduce management to achieve management-to-staff ratios, in heavy managed care environments, to 1:30.[13]

The result is that the jobs of the remaining managers are enlarged and broadened to include responsibility for larger numbers of employees and, in some cases, dissimilar departments or departments in more than one setting. Thus, those individuals who desire to continue in management roles will need to possess a broad range of skills, be very flexible, and be capable of working with employees from a variety of backgrounds and disciplines. Also, as fewer management jobs remain, particularly in hospitals, competition will heighten. Individuals desiring management work will need to explore opportunities in other settings, such as managed care, home care, physician–hospital organizations, consulting, and so on.

Figure 1-1.   The Difference between Traditional and Fully Coordinated Organizations

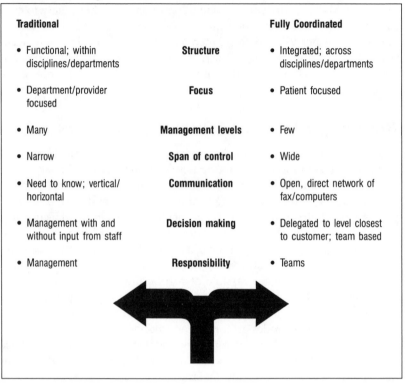

Traditional		Fully Coordinated
• Functional; within disciplines/departments	**Structure**	• Integrated; across disciplines/departments
• Department/provider focused	**Focus**	• Patient focused
• Many	**Management levels**	• Few
• Narrow	**Span of control**	• Wide
• Need to know; vertical/horizontal	**Communication**	• Open, direct network of fax/computers
• Management with and without input from staff	**Decision making**	• Delegated to level closest to customer; team based
• Management	**Responsibility**	• Teams

Consequently, now is a good time for managers and executives to complete a thorough self-assessment process to determine their interests, strengths, and developmental needs. Matching that inventory with the jobs currently available and those that are expected to develop can provide the opportunity to prepare in advance for changes in employment, whether imposed or self-initiated.

A Redefinition of Desired Worker Attributes

As the work and the workplace adopt new forms, the attributes desired in workers also are changing. The heightened need to respond rapidly to change is resulting in a shift away from specific technical skills to a greater emphasis on worker characteristics. That does not mean that technical skills are no longer important but, rather, that success and employment are not guaranteed by their possession to the same degree as in the past. One human resources manager weighs skills in this way when considering new hires: 10 percent education, 40 percent desired skill sets, and 50 percent for the ability to work productively with others.[14] In a recent hospital consolidation, characteristics identified as requirements for managers and executives included team orientation, tolerance for ambiguity, flexibility, and a systems-theory view of the organization and the work.[15] These kinds of changes may seem subtle, but they signal a shift in desired attributes of managers and workers.

In addition, many of the duties previously reserved for management are becoming the responsibility of workers. For example, workers are participating increasingly in self-managed teams, and the work of managers is shifting to broader oversight of projects or responsibility for servant leadership roles with multiple self-managed teams.

The fact is that changes are occurring in health care that are similar to those that have surfaced over the past several years in other industries. In 1993, at a Workforce Development Summit Conference in Oregon, employers agreed that the skills they used to seek in managers now were being sought in frontline workers, such as problem solving, conflict resolution, performance review, communication, and, most of all, the ability to deal with change.[16] These are all skills that also are essential to the nursing profession.

Changes Affecting Nurses in Management and Executive Practice

In health care, there are three common situations that are producing career transitions for nurse managers and executives. These are:

1. *Mergers, acquisitions, and joint operating agreements are happening with growing frequency.* As these new organizational relationships are established, it is common for management to be restructured. The number of management levels affected may vary by organization, but the executive levels are usually included. Such changes may result in a structure redesign requiring management to re-apply for positions or to take part in an appointment process. In either case, the outcome is the same: Managers leave the organization. The objective is to reduce manpower and expense, pushing dollars to the bottom line. Although severance and outplacement support are usually offered, the manager/executive may find him- or herself unemployed in short order and competing for fewer and fewer positions in the field.
2. *A transition career situation is created by the same process described above, but the manager/executive is appointed to the newly defined role.* The new responsibilities generally will include more areas

of responsibility and usually involve the consolidation of services across organizations. This is high-risk work, highly charged with political considerations, and may later result in further reorganization or management displacement.

3. *Given the turbulent environment, a manager/executive may take the initiative to find a new opportunity.* Rather than wait for the outcome of organizational restructuring, the manager may initiate a job search and leave the organization for some other opportunity.

In each case, competence is of value to the transitioning manager but is no longer a sure protection of employment. First, many other candidates may be fully capable of assuming the role in question. Second, political considerations may affect selection or the perception of performance in a given role. Consequently, managers need to continually assess the workplace dynamics and make their own assessment of their current and ongoing fit in the organization. As the organization changes over time, managers need to determine what changes are necessary on their part to remain successful in the organization or at what point they should be preparing for a transition to another organization. Thus, it is important to be current on the skills and knowledge needed to remain marketable outside the current employment situation.

One question managers need to consider is whether they view their work as a job or a career. Is the manager an employee or a free agent? Answers to these questions will determine whether a manager responds in a reactive or proactive manner toward employment. Those managers who view their work as a job and function as an employee may find themselves unemployed and unprepared for other opportunities should the employment situation change unexpectedly. Although choosing to view work as a career, and him- or herself as a free agent, offers the manager no more job security, this frame of self-reference does create a mind-set that results in the manager's being better prepared to seek other employment should the need arise. In light of the changes in health care today, it is advisable for managers to direct their careers as free agents. As such, they will work diligently to perform well in their current role, all the while surveying the field for opportunities and continually sharpening knowledge and skills to match those in demand.

Development of a Career Lifeline

You, as health care managers and nurse executives, can ensure that you are prepared for the contingency of an unexpected career transition by developing what might be called a *career lifeline.* Following are the major elements involved in this process:

- Develop your core skills and interests
- Develop your thinking
- Broaden your menu of options
- Monitor and engage the market
- Create a career center
- Remain search ready

Develop Your Core Skills and Interests

In management, certain skills are transferable and important to success regardless of the specific position you are employed to fill. Ensuring that these skills are well developed and taking steps to update or strengthen them as necessary are important to your ongoing success. This is especially true if you want to remain search ready and capable of marketing your value to potential employers. A simple but useful listing of the major categories of management skills has been developed by Baber and Waymon.[17] (See figure 1-2.) You can use these categories as a form of self-assessment by rating your current abilities as "none," "novice," "adequate," or "expert" and then setting specific goals for improvement. Of course, many other assessment tools are available for use, including formal testing. The method you use is not nearly as important as deciding to choose a method or methods and periodically completing an assessment. The information is invaluable for the manager committed to continuous improvement and lifelong learning.

Develop Your Thinking

Your mind is your most valuable asset. You should work diligently to develop your ability to think and reason. This can be accomplished by seeking intellectually stimulating experiences. It is well accepted that playing chess helps to develop logical thinking skills and the ability to develop contingency plans. One effective way to develop your mind is to read broadly within and outside your industry, as well as classical literature

Figure 1-2. Major Management Skill Categories

• Managing budgets	• Managing projects with deadlines
• Leading people	• Interviewing and briefing
• Relating to customers and other publics	• Training and coaching
• Using leading-edge technology	• Coordinating and organizing
• Writing and editing	• Influencing and negotiating

Source: Baber, A., and Waymon, L. *How to Fireproof your Career: Survival Strategies for Volatile Times.* New York City: Berkley Publishing Group, 1995, pp. 173–74.

and about new developments and sciences. Reading about chaos theory, in particular, can give you ideas about order and pattern in nature perceived as chaos, which you can compare to observations about organizations during times of chaotic change. Exploring and considering information outside your discipline can change how you think about your work. A useful way to reinforce what you have learned is to dialogue with other people in your community who have similar interests. These activities will enrich your life and stimulate your inquisitiveness. Sometimes it is surprising how exploring information outside our day-to-day work can stimulate and challenge our thinking about our work.

Broaden Your Menu of Options

Think broadly about your work and explore options that may seem far removed from your current work. For example, arrange to spend time in an insurance company and explore managed care from that side of the industry. Determine how their work is organized and carried out, what key roles exist, what is rewarding and frustrating about their work, and so on. This will accomplish two things. First, it will help you become more aware of evolving career opportunities; and second, it will enhance your knowledge about how work in different settings or industries may be interrelated or interdependent. In addition to helping you determine skills that may be necessary in a future role, this information may help you identify career opportunities elsewhere that you may wish to pursue.

Monitor and Engage the Market

Building a network of contacts over the course of your career is one of the most effective ways to monitor and continually engage the market. Most good jobs are not advertised. Who you know has more to do with your access to knowledge about the availability of an opportunity than any other factor. However, the value and effectiveness of a network depends on the effort you are willing to put into it. You must be willing to reciprocate to others within your network, which means committing regular time to making contacts and keeping in touch with people. Networking is about building relationships over time.

Some effective ways to make contacts and become known in your field include:

- Joining professional organizations such as the American Organization of Nurse Executives, the American Nurses Association, the National League for Nursing, or the American College of Healthcare Executives

- Holding state or national office in professional associations, such as committee member or chair, secretary, or president
- Writing for publication, including writing letters to the editor, abstracts, articles, or book chapters
- Speaking at local, regional, or national conferences to share your experience and expertise with others in the field
- Consulting with either others in your organization or with other organizations to share your expertise in a particular area

Although you may believe you do not have time for these types of activities, keep in mind that these are activities that you do for yourself. They help strengthen your skills as a well-rounded professional and broaden you and your sphere of influence beyond your current employment situation.

Create a Career Center

A secure career lifeline depends on your ability to function independently of your current employer. If all your resources and information about your work experience are located in your place of employment, you will be at greater risk should a transition occur suddenly. Therefore, it is to your advantage to establish your own career center at home. Although it may seem redundant to duplicate equipment or resources that you have access to at work, imagine how difficult it would be to function effectively if all that were suddenly unavailable to you. Stories abound about executives escorted from the workplace with a few boxes of personal effects. You can strengthen your ability to respond to sudden job loss by already having a personal workplace equipped and organized for your immediate use.

At a minimum, you should consider a desk, a computer, a printer, a fax machine, a file cabinet, and personal business cards as requirements for your career center. Bring copies of anything relevant to your career and experience home, even if you have copies at work. This should include, at minimum:

- A resume
- Curriculum vitae
- Performance evaluations
- Past and present job descriptions
- Letters of praise or recommendation
- Samples of your best work
- A list of educational programs you have attended
- Important addresses and phone numbers[18]

Should you experience job loss, you will be energized by the knowledge that you are fully capable of beginning a job search and do not have to waste precious energy and time on the task of getting organized. Staying prepared and organized outside the workplace will ensure that you are search ready.

Remain Search Ready

Being search ready can be of little advantage if you are unable to determine when it is time to take action, that is, when to initiate a search on your behalf. Making this determination requires careful monitoring of the health of both your current organization and the external forces affecting your employer and the industry itself. It also requires keeping up to date with your reading and maintaining your involvement in a strong network. The broader your sources of information, the more effective you will be at monitoring factors affecting your employment opportunities.

Remaining search ready involves the following:

1. *Assume that there is no job security and that your future depends on your employability.* Only you can ensure your employability; this is not something your employer will strive to accomplish on your behalf. So, take action each week to ensure your future. For example, set a goal to make one or two network contracts each week. Develop a plan for the year that specifies what your networking goals are and the specific number and types of contacts you want to make. Break this down into steps that you can execute on a weekly basis. This will take the effort out of it and support you in accomplishing your networking goal even when your work is very hectic.

2. *Watch your organization and industry carefully for signs warning of the need to take action.* Often people who experience job loss say they had no warning. Although you do not want to fixate on the possibility that your job could be in jeopardy to the extent that your ability to function effectively is impaired, you do want to watch for signs that your job may not be secure. Figure 1-3 summarizes signs of potential difficulty in the work setting, and figure 1-4 lists signs warning of potential problems with your performance. Although neither list is all-inclusive, each does provide examples of the types of signs to watch for. You should review the lists periodically, perhaps when you update your resume, and honestly assess whether you have observed any of these signs in relationship to the organization or your performance.

   If you do not see the warning signs early enough and are caught in a situation, remaining search ready will be like having

Figure 1-3. Workplace Warning Signs

• Vacant jobs left unfilled	• Overtime prohibited
• Increase in number of new hires	• Consolidation of services or offices
• Hiring freeze	• Increase in cross-training
• Rumors that early retirement will be offered	• Leadership changes, new boss

Sources: Baber, A., and Waymon, L. *How to Fireproof Your Career: Survival Strategies for Volatile Times.* New York City: Berkley Publishing Group, 1995; Morin, W. J. *Parting Company: How to Survive the Loss of a Job and Find Another Successfully.* Orlando, FL: Harcourt Brace & Company, 1991; Vestal, K. Fired! managing the process. *Journal of Nursing Administration* 20(6):14–16, 1990.

Figure 1-4. Personal Performance Warning Signs

- You are no longer invited to meetings.
- Your phone calls are not returned promptly.
- Your name is dropped from important routings.
- Your calendar has fewer meetings scheduled.
- You have frequent conflicts with peers/superiors.
- You experience less support from peers/subordinates.
- You have increasing philosophical differences with organizational policies and decisions.
- You experience unresolved role conflicts.
- Your subordinates are overused on high-level projects.
- You are unable to get appointments with superiors.
- You do not receive support for your initiatives.
- You are not promoted or do not get normal raises.
- You hate your job.
- You are not personally productive.
- You miss objectives.

Sources: Baber, A., and Waymon, L. *How to Fireproof Your Career: Survival Strategies for Volatile Times.* New York City: Berkley Publishing Group, 1995; Morin, W. J. *Parting Company: How to Survive the Loss of a Job and Find Another Successfully.* Orlando, FL: Harcourt Brace & Company, 1991; Vestal, K. Fired! managing the process. *Journal of Nursing Administration* 20(6):14–16, 1990.

an insurance policy. You will be able to start your search more quickly than those who have not taken the trouble to prepare in advance.

3. *Develop your abilities and experiences broadly.* This will give you the ability to pursue a fuller range of opportunities. For example, if you work in a hospital setting, volunteer for assignments and projects that team you with colleagues in ambulatory or home care settings. A perfect time for assessing such opportunities is when the organization is preparing for review by the Joint Commission on Accreditation of Healthcare Organizations. There is always more work to do than people feel is possible in the time available. Also, most of the standards are now integrated and rely heavily on demonstrating collaboration across disciplines and

organizational lines. As you work alongside colleagues who are skilled in areas you would like to learn more about, you will have the opportunity to learn about their side of the business. This information and experience can help you in preparing to bridge to other kinds of roles at some point in the future.

4. *Continue to cultivate a network of resources.* The list of effective ways to build and maintain contacts mentioned earlier is a wise investment in your future.

5. *Above all, focus on doing your current job well.* This is one of the best ways to keep your skills fine-tuned and to build a reputation for doing high-quality work. Competence is a portable commodity.

There are many ways to leave an organization; some will leave you exhilarated, some relieved, and some stunned. No matter the circumstance that leads to your departure, you will fare better if you are prepared in advance for the transition. You should strive to be like an athlete in training, always preparing and staying fit—in career terms, remaining search ready.

Common Questions and Answers

Following are some common questions that people have about job loss. The answers provided encapsulate much of the information in this chapter.

- *How does the term employment security differ from job security?* *Employment security* means having skills and benefits that are portable rather than having a specific job. Further, responsibility for attaining and retaining employment rests with the employee. *Job security* traditionally has been associated with an employer providing a secure job for the employee.
- *Is job security a thing of the past?* Job security in terms of the ability to hold a single job over the course of an individual's work life is indeed becoming less common. Because work in organizations is changing more rapidly today than it did in the past, employers need the flexibility to redefine jobs as needed. Those workers who are capable of responding to the changing needs of organizations will have the most success in remaining employed. However, it will be less common in the future for job security to be achieved by retaining the same position. *Employability*, the ability to obtain employment by demonstrating your value to an employer, will be key to achieving employment security.
- *Why do organizations need fewer managers? Should I be preparing for a nonmanagement job in the future?* Partly because of the nature of work in an information society and partly because of the rapidity of change, decision making and action must be placed close to the customer or point of service. Thus, workers are being given more autonomy to act, and there is less need for hierarchy in organizations, which means there is less need for managers. The jobs of the remaining managers are broadened to include responsibility for larger numbers of employees and, in some cases, dissimilar departments or departments in more than one setting. To prepare for these changes, managers should assess the skills needed to manage in the new environment and work to strengthen their skills as necessary to compete for fewer management jobs. If a manager has an interest in pursuing nonmanagement roles and possesses the necessary skill sets, his or her employability would be enhanced.
- *What will it take to continue in a management role in today's health care environment?* Managers and executives who desire to continue in management roles will need to possess a broad range of skills, to be very flexible, and to be capable of working with employees from a variety of backgrounds and disciplines. As fewer management jobs remain, particularly in hospitals, competition will

heighten. Individuals desiring management work will need to explore opportunities in other settings, such as managed care, home care, physician–hospital organizations, consulting, and so on. Now is a good time for managers and executives to complete a thorough self-assessment process to determine interests, strengths, and developmental needs. Matching the inventory with jobs currently available and those that are expected to develop can provide the opportunity to prepare in advance for changes in employment, whether imposed or self-initiated.

- *What should I be doing now to protect myself in case I lose my job?* You should focus on three major areas: developing your core skills and interests, developing your ability to think and reason, and building a network of contacts. The first two focus on building your capability, and the last one on monitoring and engaging the market. Having marketable skills and being aware of employment opportunities are equally important to employment security.

- *What are the most common situations that produce career transitions for nurse managers and executives?* The three most common situations in health care that are producing transitions for nurse managers and executives are job loss due to restructuring, appointment to a newly structured role, and self-initiated job change. In all three cases, the predominant stimulus for change comes as a result of organizational changes such as mergers, acquisitions, and joint operating agreements.

- *Why isn't it enough to just be competent anymore?* First, there are more competent and capable candidates for fewer jobs. Political considerations also may affect selection or perception of performance in a given role. Managers need to assess the workplace dynamics continually and to make their own assessment of their current and ongoing fit in the organization. It is important to remain current on skills and knowledge needed to be marketable outside the present employment situation.

- *What types of career information and documents should I keep at home, and how often should I update them?* Keep copies of anything relevant to your career and experience at home, even if you have copies at work. This includes your resume, curriculum vitae, performance evaluations, past and present job descriptions, letters of praise or recommendation, samples of your best work, a list of educational programs you have attended, important addresses and numbers, and so on. You should update your resume and curriculum vitae each quarter. An easy way to accomplish this goal is by recording relevant information as it occurs and dropping a note in a file or a log that can be used when you do your updates. As far as updating home files, the easiest thing to do is to bring items home as they are completed. This step allows you to keep your files current with minimal effort.

- *What are some signs that my job may not be secure?* First, you may notice changes in the workplace such as vacant jobs being left unfilled, an increase in the number of new hires, a hiring freeze, rumors about early retirement, prohibited overtime, a consolidation of services, and changes in leadership. Second, you may observe warning signs that indicate potential problems with your performance, including changes in your inclusion in normal workplace activities, conflicts with peers or superiors, unresolved role conflicts, reduced access to information or superiors, and loss of personal productivity.

- *How can behaving as a free agent protect my employability?* The most important way is by affecting your mind-set about employment. You are more likely to be successful in your current job and capable of obtaining a new job if you see yourself as manager of your career. This type of mind-set positions you for action.

- *I recently lost my job after working for the same organization for 20 years. Where do I begin?* You would benefit from outplacement assistance if it is available to you. Trained professionals are available through the service to assist you in determining the goals of your job search, writing a resume and cover letters, and preparing for interviews, as well as to support your efforts during the job search process. If you do not have access to outplacement services, contact colleagues who have held more than one job and who have had experience with the job search process. A colleague can effectively mentor you during the process.

References

1. Wheatley, M. *Leadership and the New Sciences: Learning about Organization from an Orderly Universe.* San Francisco: Berret-Koehler, 1994.

2. Baber, A., and Waymon, L. *How to Fireproof Your Career: Survival Strategies for Volatile Times.* New York City: Berkley Publishing Group, 1995, p. 27.

3. Baber and Waymon, p. 3.

4. Stearns, A. K. *Living through Job Loss: Coping with the Emotional Effects of Job Loss and Rebuilding Your Future.* New York City: Simon and Schuster, 1995, p. 141.

5. Baber and Waymon, p. 98.

6. Filipczak, B. You're on your own: training, employability, and the new employment contract. *Training* 32:30, Jan. 1995.

7. Baber and Waymon, p. 4.

8. Baber and Waymon, p. 6.

9. Leonard, B. Downsized & out: career survival in the '90s. *HRMagazine,* 40(6):92, June 1995.

10. Stearns, p. 163.

11. Stearns, p. 167.

12. Baber and Waymon, p. 28.

13. K. Vestal, The Hay Group, Dallas, personal communication, 1996.

14. Stearns, p. 158.

15. Vestal.

16. Stearns, p. 161.

17. Baber and Waymon, p. 173.

18. Baber and Waymon, pp. 230–31.

Bibliography

Andrica, D. C. Networking: to do or not to do and how to. *Nursing Economics* 12(5):284, Sept.–Oct, 1994.

Baber, A., and Waymon, L. *How to Fireproof Your Career: Survival Strategies for Volatile Times.* New York City: Berkley Publishing Group, 1995.

Beckham, J. D. The death of management. *Healthcare Forum Journal,* 38(4):14–22, Jul.–Aug. 1995.

Block, P. *Stewardship: Choosing Service over Self-Interest.* San Francisco: Berrett-Koehler Publishers, 1993.

Bridges, W. *Job*Shift: *How to Prosper in a Workplace without Jobs.* New York City: Addison-Wesley, 1994.

Bruce, R. C. *Executive Job Search Strategies: The Guide for Career Transitions.* Lincolnwood, IL: VGM Career Horizons, 1994.

Burton, M. L., and Wedemeyer, R. A. *In Transition.* New York City: HarperCollins, 1991.

Criscito, P. *Designing the Perfect Resume.* New York City: Barron's, 1995.

Corbin, B., and Wright, S. *The Edge: Resume & Job Search Strategy.* Carmel, IN: Beckett-Highland, 1993.

Filipczak, B. You're on your own: training, employability, and the new employment contract. *Training* 32:29–36, Jan. 1995.

Hyatt, C., and Gottlieb, L. *When Smart People Fail: Rebuilding Yourself for Success.* New York City: Penguin, 1993.

Leonard, B. Downsized & out: career survival in the '90s. *HRMagazine*, 40(6):89–92, June 1995.

Mills, D. Q. *Rebirth of the Corporation.* New York City: John Wiley & Sons, 1993.

Morin, W. J. *Parting Company: How to Survive the Loss of a Job and Find Another Successfully.* Orlando, FL: Harcourt Brace & Company, 1991.

Stearns, A. K. *Living through Job Loss: Coping with the Emotional Effects of Job Loss and Rebuilding Your Future.* New York City: Simon & Schuster, 1995.

Unger, P. Culture shock: tips for transitioners. *Management Review,* 84(6):44–47, June 1995.

Vestal, K. Fired! managing the process. *Journal of Nursing Administration* 20(6):14–16, June 1990.

Wheatley, M. *Leadership and the New Science: Learning about Organization from an Orderly Universe.* San Francisco: Berret-Koehler, 1994.

Chapter 2

Coping with Job Loss

Julie Klausen Moe, MSN, RN

A lmost everyone who loses a job experiences shock, embarrassment, anger, and some degree of depression. Add to this the many practical and financial problems associated with finding a new job, and the experience can seem overwhelming. Senior executives react much the same as middle managers. Regardless of the position or the circumstances of the termination, most people struggle with feelings of failure and rejection and feel as though they have lost control of their lives.

Although it may seem like it at the time, the loss of a job is not the end of the world. It is possible to transform what feels like a crushing defeat into a victory, both personally and professionally. Many who survive a job loss report feeling much more confident and competent in the end. Even though it is impossible to avoid the pain and anger that accompany a termination, it is possible to manage those feelings and move ahead positively and productively. It is even possible to find a new job that can prove to be more interesting, satisfying, and financially rewarding than the previous position. Job searching is demanding and at times emotionally challenging, but there is no mysterious process involved. Those people who take care of themselves, both emotionally and physically, and plan their search carefully *will* find another position.

This chapter describes the termination process and offers suggestions on how to manage the exit from your previous position, cope with your emotional responses, and improve your attitude in order to move forward with your job search and your life.

Dealing with the Termination Process

Chances are that, in your formal educational training, you never learned how it feels to be fired. You probably never learned about it from your family or friends, either. However, despite the fact that most of us have little knowledge of or practice in the termination experience, it is a significant event in our lives and should be explored. It is important to understand what will happen, how you will most likely react, and, most important, how you should respond to being terminated.

How Terminations Are Conducted

Organizations may or may not have well-thought-out plans for terminations. Often the process is not accomplished in a sensitive and professional manner. If you are treated well, consider yourself fortunate. Whatever the process, try not to take it personally. Feeling angry over the methods used to terminate you is a waste of energy you will need to cope with your situation.

Group layoffs usually are announced at a predetermined time, and those responsible for delivering the news often have received training on how to proceed. However, if your boss is faced with a single individual termination, he or she may not be trained and may delay the confrontation for days or even weeks. As time passes, the anxiety your boss feels will grow, causing him or her to terminate you in either of two extreme manners.

On the one hand, your boss's pent-up anxiety may result in an insensitive, even cruel termination. He or she may attribute the decision to others in the organization or may try to coerce a confession of guilt or failure out of you. Discussion will be minimal, and you may leave the meeting without really understanding the reasons for your termination. On the other hand, your boss may wander off in the other direction and never get to the point. He or she will beat around the bush and make ineffective attempts to bring up the topic of termination. Finally, your boss may never succeed and decide to send you to the Human Resources department in the hope that someone there will deliver the bad news. Eventually, however, you will get the message from someone, and as soon as you realize you have lost your job, you will most likely be assaulted by disturbing emotions.

Common Reactions to Being Terminated

Regardless of the termination tactics or the number of staff affected, you probably will feel as if you have lost control of your life. According to W. J. Morin and J. C. Cabrera, people who have been terminated tend to react in one of the following ways:[1]

- *Anticipation:* If you have heard rumors of restructuring or downsizing or have assessed that the danger signs discussed in chapter 1 apply to you, you may be anticipating your termination. Although you will still be upset when it actually occurs, the termination will not come as a shock, and your reactions will likely be somewhat buffered by having your suspicions confirmed. Despite feelings of disappointment—even anger, fear, and shame—you are more likely to accept your termination as a real, if unpleasant, fact of life. The anticipation reaction is characterized by the relative ease with which you accept your fate and cope with your emotions. In this case, the termination interview should be less intense and you will be able to concentrate on the practical matters related to a severance package and your future.

- *Disbelief:* If you have *not* anticipated your termination, your reaction is likely to be one of disbelief. You will feel completely shocked and say things such as "They can't do this to me" or "This can't be happening to me." You may even plead for your job or another position in the company. Some employees experiencing this reaction become numb and unresponsive, and find it difficult to do anything, even talk. In this case, the termination interview will likely be intense and unproductive.

- *Escape:* In this case, you understand what has happened to you but do not know what to do next and decide flight is the best option. Some people choose to escape to the nearest bar or liquor store—definitely not a good choice. If escape is your reaction to being terminated, you may end up leaving the termination interview before you understand the reasons for your termination or the terms of your severance package.

- *Euphoria:* It is possible to respond to the news as if you are delighted to hear that you have been terminated. More likely, you are just relieved that the waiting is over. Even though the euphoria is usually short-lived, some people report that the uncertainty of not knowing whether they will be laid off is more stressful than the reality of termination.

- *Violence:* The reaction feared most by both those being terminated and those doing the terminating is violence. In fact, this is the least common response to termination. Almost everyone feels some degree of anger at being terminated, but most people are able to control their emotions. If there is violence during a termination interview, it is usually verbal with raised voices and threats of lawsuits.[2] Obviously, violence obstructs any meaningful communication during the termination meeting.

If you feel you may lose control and do something that may harm you or someone around you, get professional help immediately. Contact your physician, for example, or a mental health professional. Although this reaction to job loss is rare, it must be taken seriously.

Initial Emotional Reactions to Being Terminated

Job loss is the third most severe loss people can suffer after death of a loved one and divorce.[3] In many ways, the emotional turmoil following a job loss is very similar to that following death or divorce. For example, the newly unemployed also experience a cycle of grief and loss. Studies have shown that the newly unemployed said the experience was, in the beginning, worse than they had feared. In addition to the trauma of having to find another job, they are confronted with many unanticipated and disturbing emotions, including shock at being out of work, hurt and anger at having been betrayed by their company, and finally, embarrassment at having to tell parents, partners, and children that they have lost their jobs.

Although it is difficult to predict exactly how anyone will react to losing a job, many people report that several, or frequently all, of the following emotions surfaced almost immediately after they learned they had been terminated:[4]

- *Anger:* You feel furious that someone has just taken something of great value to you—your job. You feel as though you have tremendous amounts of time and energy invested in this organization, and you have been treated unfairly.
- *Shame:* You have lost something valuable and may think it is your own fault. Many who are terminated chastise themselves ruthlessly. Even in companies that are downsizing large numbers of employees, people often feel stupid for not having foreseen their termination and for not avoiding it. They blame themselves for not positioning themselves well enough or for not having worked harder. Also, they feel ashamed in front of family and friends.
- *Fear:* A main part of the structure in your life has been suddenly taken away from you, and the consequences are unknown. You wonder how you will pay bills, how your family and friends will react, and how, or if, you will ever find another job. Worst-case scenarios race through your mind.
- *Sadness:* Losing your job is cause for grief and mourning. Not only will you never have the same job with this organization again, you will be leaving friends and coworkers.
- *Self-pity:* You probably will feel as if you do not deserve to be terminated and wonder why you have been singled out for this fate. A common response is, "How could they do this to me?"

By understanding that these emotions are normal and expected, you may be able to work through them more effectively.

The emotions listed above are by no means the only ones you will experience following a job loss. You may react in other ways, and that is okay. You have every right to feel any emotion. However, what is important is the ability to accept your individual emotional reactions so that you can move on. The next step is to determine your response to the news of your termination.

How to Negotiate the Termination Process

The best response to your termination is to keep your feelings in control. Although you cannot control how you feel, you can control how you respond. You must take control of this very negative incident and turn it into a positive, or at least neutral, situation. Restrained, professional conduct is called for even under difficult circumstances. Professional conduct can positively affect your chances of securing a new position. Your current employer can be invaluable in your job search by offering a formal recommendation and use of his or her informal network.

Taking Time to Take Stock

Some experts believe that the best response to the news of termination is simply to leave, not in an emotional "I've got to get out of here" escape but, instead, in a calm, controlled manner.[5,6] You might tell your boss that the decision has taken you by surprise and you need time to think over how things might best be handled. Explain that you want your transition out of the organization to be positive, make an appointment with him or her for the next day, and then calmly leave the termination interview. Unless you feel very sure of yourself, postponing this discussion a day makes good sense. A postponement will give you time to deal with your initial emotions, and most important, it will help deter you from doing or saying anything that you might regret later as you move forward with your career.

In return for your cooperation in this process, you will benefit. Remember that your severance package (if one is provided) is offered to "guarantee" your professional handling of this change. If you create havoc in the organization, the organization's incentive to provide transitional support is greatly diminished. Even if severance is not an issue, professional conduct during this time will always be beneficial to your future.

Another important thing to remember during the termination process is that you should not become a victim. The time to manage the process is while you are involved in it, not later through the courts. The worst possible mismanagement of the process is to let your emotions provoke you into storming out of the company. If you do, you will leave with few options to manage the process and you may have closed the door on a reasonable job transition package.

Clarifying the Transition Package

One of the first things you need to clarify is what the organization is prepared to do for you. This involves knowing the details of the severance package (if one is provided), including how much severance you will be provided and how it will be paid. You also need to determine the status of your fringe benefits, including medical coverage, reimbursement for unused vacation and sick leave, profit sharing, the pension plan, and club memberships, if applicable. Further, you should find out if the company will provide support for your job search, including office/secretarial support and career counseling/outplacement. (See chapter 4 for a discussion of severance agreements.)

Determining the Causes of Termination

Beyond the practical severance issues, you should attempt to determine as accurately as possible what caused your termination. You need to know this information, not because you might save your job but because it will help you plan for the future. You need to ask the question, even if the answer may be unpleasant.

Deciding Whether to Seek Outside Advice

An important decision during this time will be whether to contact an attorney for advice or management of the termination process. If you clearly understand what you want and have good negotiating skills, you may not need outside counsel. If, however, you have no idea what executives usually get in such circumstances, get help. In case you consider this advice antimanagement, remember that few executives let themselves be terminated without acquiring the best legal advice they can.[7] Nurse executives typically ask for little severance upon leaving, in contrast to other executives in health care who negotiate extensive severance packages.[8]

Saying Good-Bye to Colleagues

A professional exit also includes allowing the organization's members to say good-bye to you. To the extent possible under the circumstances and within the given time frame, you should follow the strategies outlined in figure 2-1. It is advisable for you to communicate additional projects to be done and any pending items in writing, and to keep a copy for your personal file. Doing so should help avoid any confusion or miscommunication concerning the transition of responsibilties. Further, this written copy can be utilized defensively should future litigation arise concerning allegations of projects not completed or issues not

Figure 2-1. Business Strategies for a Professional Exit

- Assist the replacement person as much as feasible before the actual exit.
- Tell the boss what remains unaccomplished.
- Sum up any crucial ideas or responsible items pending.
- Stay in touch as appropriate to keep the source of recommendation open and positive.

Source: Blouin, A. S., and Brent, N. J. Nurse administrators in job transition: managing the exit. *Journal of Nursing Administration* 22(10):12, Oct. 1992.

attended to during your tenure.[9] In addition, you should obtain copies of successfully completed projects executed while you were employed in the organization. Most companies will allow you to do so unless the information is seen as proprietary or confidential.

If your exit allows for time to say good-bye colleagues and complete unfinished business, it is important that you do so in a manner that is consistent with the terms of your severance agreement, if one is used. For example, most agreements typically contain clauses stating that both parties must maintain confidentiality concerning the exit and the specifics of the severance package and that an agreed-upon reason for leaving (for example, career advancement) be given. You must adhere to those provisions because failure to do so may threaten the entire package.[10] Even if you are not bound by a formal severance agreement, it is wise to refrain from bad-mouthing the organization or anyone in it so that you can leave on a positive, professional note. The period from the time you learn of your termination to the time you leave the office is an extremely important interval. Until you exit for good, you should evaluate every action for its potential impact on your job search and future career.

Coping Postexit

During the first several days after learning of your termination, you have two immediate priorities. These are to:

1. Deal with your emotions
2. Consider several practical survival issues

Tackling these issues helps you orient yourself away from the past and toward the future. During the first 72 hours posttermination, you should concentrate on understanding and accepting what has happened so that you can begin to devote your energies to the practical business of finding a new job.

Some career management experts would advise you to do nothing initially. Your immediate impulse is likely to be a frantic need to find a job and to do it quickly. However, you should resist the temptation to immediately call business associates or consult recruitment firms because you probably are not ready to make your best impression at this time. Instead, the more prudent action is to assess the situation, think about why you were terminated, list possible options for the future, and then create a plan to fit your assessment.[11]

Work through Your Emotions

As mentioned earlier, job loss is an experience in bereavement. Shock, sadness, insomnia, loss of appetite, anger, self-doubt or self-blame, anxiety, and depression are all symptoms of the grief and healing process brought on by your personal crisis. These are normal emotional reactions which you can understand, work through, and move beyond.[12]

Before you are ready to start your job search, you must first deal with your emotions. Although it is best to control your emotions during the termination interview, once you have left your place of employment, it is vital to vent them. Share your feelings and thoughts with someone you can trust. For people who are married, a spouse typically is the obvious choice of confidant, although not the sole option. In some cases, spouses feel so threatened and upset about the loss of a job that they are unable to provide the calm, understanding assistance their partners need. If this is the case in your situation, consider talking to a close friend, a member of the clergy, or perhaps a professional vocational counselor, psychologist, or psychiatrist. Seeking help is not a sign of weakness but, rather, a sign of strength. It indicates your intention to improve your situation rather than wallowing in your misfortune. At this stage, your goal is to work through your intense feelings and ultimately compose yourself so that you can determine your best course of action for the future. Whether your confidant is a professional or not, he or she should be someone who is willing to listen, draw out your feelings, and offer support. A supportive listener will not make judgments about how you feel, nor will he or she offer you a laundry list of suggestions. As much as possible, you should avoid choosing a confidant who will be more likely to dispense advice than to listen to you talk about your loss.

Taking a little time for psychic repair after experiencing a job loss will enable you to have a more positive attitude, be happier, and be more productive at your next place of employment. People who shed the negatives of the past are psychologically better able to forge a successful future for themselves.[13] However, people who hold in their negative feelings are likely to see them resurface during the course of the job search, causing them both personal and professional problems. Bottled-up anger will come through in job interviews no matter how well hidden you may think it is. Even worse, unacknowledged feelings of loss can grow. In the early weeks and months following a personal crisis such as a job loss, people often deny the full impact of the loss, ignoring the extent of their hurt, anger, or concern. Experiencing a threat to their self-image, competence, and status, many individuals use denial as a coping mechanism. Although the mechanisms of inaction and avoidance may protect you from this threat, they do not help you deal with the problem. Keeping up defenses requires a lot of energy and leads to increased fatigue, tension, and anxiety.[14]

The venting process is as individual as your emotions and will vary in length for different people. However, the more feelings that surface during this process, the better. Talking about your feelings will prevent you from becoming overwhelmed by them, and at some point you will see a change in your reactions. You will notice that your thoughts are beginning to shift from a focus on the past to a focus on the future, from what has happened to what you need to do next. If this does not occur by the end of a week or two, you may need to look more closely at your situation. It may be that you are procrastinating, maintaining the status quo for as long as possible; or you may find that, rather than confronting and venting your emotions, you are burying them. If this happens, you should contact a professional counselor to help you deal with your emotions so that you can move forward with your life.[15]

You should also seek out professional help if you find that after having thoroughly vented your emotions with family or friends, you still have deep feelings of anger. Feeling angry over your loss is a normal and acceptable reaction, acting out your feelings of anger is not. Be alert to warning signs such as difficulty sleeping, loss of appetite, or depression. Seek help if you cannot shake feelings of hopelessness and anxiety or if you have thoughts of death or revenge. Unrestrained anger can disrupt and ruin lives—injuring personal relationships; leading to alcohol or drug abuse; making you ill or accident prone; contributing to depression, anxiety, and suicide; and even producing actions that can result in your arrest.[16]

Finally, work to develop strategies for releasing your anger in healthy and productive ways. Such strategies might include walking away from situations that upset you, doing physical exercise, calling a friend to let off steam, trying deep-breathing and relaxation techniques, writing an angry letter and then tearing it up, or using prayer. Do whatever works to calm you. It also is good idea to avoid drinking alcohol, because alcohol disinhibits, which can often lead to aggression.

Consider Practical Issues

When you begin to shift from dealing with your emotions to more practical issues, your first concerns are likely to revolve primarily around family and finances.

Family Issues

You should tell your spouse or partner about your termination soon after it occurs. It is important not to withhold this news from your spouse because he or she can be a great source of comfort and strength. Once the initial emotional trauma has subsided somewhat, you should make other good friends and family members aware of your circumstances, particularly children. If left to their own imagination and interpretation of your changed mood, children are likely to assume the worst.

Ideally, your loved ones will support and encourage you through this time of transition. However, it is possible that for them the job loss will be as traumatic as it is for you, or even more so, in which case your immediate family members may be unable to provide the support you need. Divorce increases among unemployed workers, and the wives of unemployed men are likely to show high levels of depression. Some spouses become resentful, blaming, rejecting, and openly hostile. Some children may become clinging, demand more attention, or experience sleep problems, accident proneness, and behavioral problems.[17,18] Your immediate family members also need to express their feelings and to be reassured that they will be taken care of. In order to provide this reassurance, you may need to seek out the support of and encouragement from other family members, friends, or professionals. It may even be necessary to obtain family counseling. Psychological distress is contagious, often moving through a family like a virus.

It should be emphasized that most families are able to cope effectively with job loss. The best protection against any kind of family stress, including a parent out of work, is family cohesion, support, and communication.[19,20] The best thing you can do during your job search is to communicate openly and frequently with your family. Take steps to develop unity and togetherness. Share with them what you are doing and what you plan to do. Make them a part of your team. And above all, listen to each other. Like you, your spouse and children need to share their feelings and fears.

Financial Issues

Your second immediate practical concern is your financial status. You will need to consider the details of your severance package, if one is provided, as well as your personal financial needs. For many people, financial issues constitute the most terrifying aspect of losing a job. Whereas the emotional stress of termination can make you angry or sad, fiscal uncertainty can make you frightened. As you plan to move forward with your job search, you obviously will need to factor financial needs and resources into the decision-making process. At the same time, however, you want to avoid the distraction of imagined financial concerns.

To avoid imagining financial disaster, you must first assess your current situation. You will need a variety of documents to perform a financial analysis, including those listed in figure 2-2. Following are some steps to take:

1. *Complete the financial statement form.* This form is a summary of assets and liabilities. Your goal is to document on paper a complete picture of what you own and owe so that you can see what you have to work with.
2. *Add up your assets.* Assess whether you have anything you can sell in the event you need to raise money immediately. Identify the worth of your major assets, including stocks, real estate, jewelry, antiques, coin collections, and so on. Also, determine whether you have items you can borrow against, such as paid-up insurance policies. Assess the availability or liquidity of your assets. Write down how long it will take to get at the money represented by your assets.
3. *List your liabilities.* If you are a home owner, separate out your mortgage and add up the total amount you owe. Consider ways you might reduce your liabilities. Your mortgage probably is your largest single monthly expenditure, so it makes sense to consider it first. Can you refinance to lower your monthly payments? Discuss the possibility with banks and mortgage brokers, and then weigh the cost of refinancing against the potential savings. Examine other debts as well. Consider selling items you are still

Figure 2-2. Data for Financial Analysis

- A financial statement form (available from your bank)
- A copy of your most recent income tax documents
- Information about your stock plans, 401(k), and other savings
- Credit card bills for the past year
- Canceled checks for the past year
- Insurance information, including home, car, life, and disability
- Information about outstanding loans (car, mortgage, school, home equity)

Source: Baber, A. K. *How to Fireproof Your Career: Survival Strategies for Volatile Times.* New York City: Berkley Publishing Group, 1995, p. 122.

paying for, such as a car, a boat, or a motor home. To further manage your debt, you should immediately eliminate any new credit buying.

4. *Determine your income and expenses.* A substantial portion of net worth is most likely connected directly to employment, so it is important to reevaluate income in light of your job loss. Write down all household income, including severance benefits, unemployment benefits, and your spouse's income. Then identify all your expenses, both periodic (for example, car insurance) and monthly (for example, mortgage). Circle all those that are vital. Finally, look at ways to augment your income and reduce your expenses. If your spouse is not currently employed, now might be the time for him or her to start. You also might consider having a garage sale, which can generate hundreds of dollars in a short period of time. In terms of minimizing your expenses, you might contact your electric and gas companies to see if they will perform free audits to show ways to reduce use. Cut back on spending for luxury items such as club memberships, magazine subscriptions, meals in restaurants, and cable TV. Finally, add up your bare-necessity monthly expenses to determine how much money you will need to live on.

   Another way to categorize your monthly expenditures is to divide them into three groups: fixed (rent, mortgage, car payments, utilities), flexible (food, clothing, education), and frills (entertainment, club memberships, vacation). Remember, even some of the fixed expenses can be lowered and some items in the flexible category can be transferred to the frills category.[21]

5. *Obtain sound, independent advice about your finances.* Experts report that most individuals fail to investigate their finances in detail and to make plans for the future until they are forced to do so, frequently when faced with a job loss. Obtaining independent financial advice probably should be your next step. As you plan your job search, it will be reassuring to know that you can focus your attention on the task ahead without having to contend with difficult financial issues.

   If you do not already have a financial advisor, many banks and brokerage firms offer financial planning services, and there are large national corporations devoted exclusively to providing such services. You want someone who is committed to serving your best interests, not someone who is pushing whatever investment offers the highest sales commission that month. Your accountant, lawyer, friends, relatives, or business associates may be able to refer you to a respected advisor. (See figure 2-3 for a list of questions to ask when interviewing a financial advisor.)

Figure 2-3. Questions to Ask Your Financial Advisor

- What areas does your financial planning service include (goal setting, tax planning, managing monthly expenses, budgeting, choosing an investment strategy, assessing insurance needs, determining liquidity of assets)?
- Can you help me think through creative alternatives to minimize the impact of a short- or long-term interruption of my income?
- What degrees and certifications have you earned?
- How are you compensated (fee only, commission only, fee and commission, or fee offset)?
- Will you provide references from past and present clients?

Source: Baber, A. K. *How to Fireproof Your Career: Survival Strategies for Volatile Times.* New York City: Berkley Publishing Group, 1995, p. 127.

A financial advisor can help you decide what to do about credit card debt, how best to utilize severance pay, how to manage and protect your assets and savings, and so on. You also can obtain free budget counseling and other valuable help from the National Consumer Credit Service.[22]

6. *Create your plan.* You will want to determine the approximate date that you need to be reemployed before wiping out all your resources. When planning, there are only three things you can do about your money: spend less, earn more, and/or manage better.[23] To spend less, consider the Depression-era motto: "Use it up, wear it out, make it do, or do without." To earn more, consider taking part-time or temporary employment, consulting, teaching, or writing. To manage better, make a list of your monthly expenses and, beginning with the largest expense, design a reduction plan. Make every penny count.

Focusing on the details of your finances can make it easy to think of them as the driving forces, or even the only factor, as you consider your job search. Although your general financial situation can play an important role in determining the career options that are open to you and although you will have to deal with your financial realities, try not to let the situation take control of your life. You might have to adapt your strategy and tactics such as taking a temporary job you do not really want as a first step toward creating your future, but consider all your options before you make a career decision.

Managing Your Emotions and Attitude

Coping during your job search is a process of effectively managing your emotions and attitude. If you implement strategies to handle your emotions and take charge of your attitude, you will survive, and even grow, through the experience of job transition.

The Effect of Job Loss on Self-Identity

Many of us, particularly in the United States, confuse what we do for a living with who we are. Consequently, when we lose our job, we feel as though we have lost our identity. Organizations sometimes encourage this kind of thinking when they require more and more hours of their employees each day. It is not uncommon in today's competitive health care market, for example, for the organization to demand that people work late most nights and come in on weekends. A disproportionate amount of time spent on the job can make you feel as if you have no identity except your work identity and no friends except your work friends. Further, this situation can weaken your relationship with your family as well as decrease the time you have to network or gain educational or professional credentials that might enhance your future marketability. When you place too much emphasis on your work, you can become extremely vulnerable and create a situation in which, if you are terminated, you experience the most profound sense of betrayal.

Researchers have identified seven key meanings of work that can explain why job loss commonly produces significant levels of anxiety and distress. They have found that work:

1. Enables us to structure our time
2. Provides a source of identity
3. Gives us relationships outside our nuclear family
4. Provides a source of obligatory activity
5. Enables us to develop skills and creativity
6. Provides a sense of purpose
7. Furnishes us with a source of income so we can exercise control in our lives[24]

Thus, what we do for a living can determine how we view ourselves — our self-concept, self-confidence, self-worth, and self-esteem — as well as how we are viewed by others. Our feelings of self-worth can be stripped away the moment we are laid off unless we free ourselves from equating work with worth.[25]

The Effect of Job Loss on Your Health

The stress of job loss and job search can make you sick, both physically and emotionally. Studies of individuals who have experienced job loss report a host of physical and emotional problems. (See figure 2-4.) But

Figure 2-4.   Physical/Emotional Problems Associated with Job Loss

- Depression
- Headaches
- Sleep disorders
- Digestive disturbances
- Fatigue

- Backaches
- Irritability
- Increased colds, flus, and infections
- Hypertension

Source: Stearns, A. K. *Living Through Job Loss: Coping with the Emotional Effects of Job Loss and Rebuilding Your Future.* New York: Simon & Schuster, 1995, pp. 87–92.

the good news is that illness is not inevitable. You do not have to become a victim. Many physical symptoms are simply a normal part of the grieving process and will diminish with time. Most long-term health risks associated with job loss can be avoided entirely or overcome.[26] Your ability to cope with your emotions and your self-care strategies can make a difference in your health during the job search.

Strategies for Managing Your Emotions

Coping begins with recognizing and learning how to manage your symptoms of distress. In addition to venting your thoughts, emotions, and plans with a confidant (family, friend, or professional counselor), you should consider the following strategies to cope with the emotional ups and downs of your job search.

Exercise Regularly

Research shows that regular physical exercise such as aerobic walking affects brain chemistry, improves circulation, reduces cholesterol levels, and lowers the risk of heart disease. Regular exercise during your job search will help you alleviate frustration, stress, worry, and anger, as well as increase your energy level and help you sleep better, look better, and feel more in control.[27,28] A physical conditioning program does not have to be strenuous in order to be effective. Just choose an activity that you enjoy and that will help you take your mind off problems. Walking, jogging, and bicycling are examples of relatively inexpensive ways to increase your activity level.

In addition to physical exercise, other activities that can be helpful in managing stress include cleaning a closet or garage, washing windows, painting a room, gardening, or maintaining the lawn. Whenever you take an action that brings more order or pleasure to your life, you help yourself to manage your emotions and reduce your level of helplessness. If necessary, begin with small projects or short periods of exercise and gradually mobilize yourself for more.

Keep a Journal

Writing is another strategy for easing the pain of job loss and boosting new job prospects. In a study of 42 unemployed, middle-aged professionals, psychologists found that members of the group who wrote about their job loss in a journal were twice as likely to have a full-time job 8 months later as those in the nonwriting group. The two groups had similar job search activity levels.[29] Therapists frequently recommend keeping a diary or journal as a means of releasing tension, gaining perspective, and achieving increased control over your destiny. Writing is a way of putting problems into a form that can make them more manageable and understandable. Write for 20 to 30 minutes at a time, stating specifically what is troubling you (not just recording day-to-day events) and date the entries. This will help you keep track of your progress. Most people are surprised and encouraged to observe the peace they are making with painful events. Holding to a strict timetable for making entries is not necessary and may only frustrate you. At the beginning, set a reachable goal of perhaps three times per week.

Some job search experts recommend keeping a career journal to document your plans and actions as well as your feelings. A career journal assists you in evaluating your progress and monitoring your performance.[30] In addition to recording thoughts and feelings, you can use it to document your job search plan, your daily activities, and your progress toward reaching your goals.

Do Volunteer Work

Self-esteem is inextricably connected to competency and meaningful work. But work does not have to be narrowly defined as that which brings home a paycheck. Broaden your definition of work to include anything that is being productive or any activity you find fulfilling.[31] Volunteering is a great way to remain productive as you continue your job search. There are as many ways to benefit from volunteering as there are activities to do. For example, you can offer to help nonprofit organizations in the arts, child health and welfare, drug prevention, the environment, social services, and many other worthwhile causes, including working with community youth programs, area churches, or your child's school.

Volunteering can actually benefit you as much as it does the recipients of your efforts. When you offer time and energy, you can reduce your tension, feel better about yourself, and also further your job search. It provides a way to make new contacts. The people you meet can spread the word about your ability, availability, and positive attitude. Making yourself useful by volunteering is an important way to regain self-respect.

Join a Support Group

A great way to help yourself and others in your situation is to either start or participate in a local support group for unemployed people in your area. The meetings would give all the participants an opportunity to describe the details of their job loss experiences and to share their feelings, both initially and currently. You can give and receive emotional encouragement and keep each other motivated.

Put Structure Back into Your Life

People who find ways to put structure back into their lives actively help themselves and others reduce stress and regain a feeling of wholeness. One way to do this is to establish a daily routine, scheduling activities and taking specific break times. Make a list of job-related tasks to be carried out daily, such as making six contact calls, writing a cover letter, or mailing an application.

Appreciate Your Talents

Another helpful activity is to list your strengths, talents, and accomplishments. This could be incorporated into your journal work. Be sure to include things you have done for other people in addition to work-related achievements. The list might include specific tasks you have done well in previous jobs, major difficulties you have overcome, and personal qualities that have led to success in the past.

Other ways to lift your spirits include taking up a hobby, listening to uplifting music, enjoying a sport, and staying away from negative or critical people who seem to cause you more grief. Maximize the time you spend with people who treat you well and respectfully.

Change Your Way of Thinking

To whatever extent you have had a tendency in the past to think that your worth as a person is determined by the work you do, the amount of money you make, or even whether you have a job at all, it is now time to reexamine these fundamental assumptions. The people who really care about you do not love you because of how much money you make, how fancy your office is, or how impressive your material acquisitions are. What is really important is far more basic—the type of person you are. Do you care about other people? Are you a person of integrity? Do you stand by people in time of need? These are the qualities that define you as a human being. These things are easy to forget, but it is vital to your emotional growth to continually remind yourself of them.

Develop a Good Job Search Attitude

Coping successfully with unemployment requires constant attention to your attitude. It is natural to doubt your abilities if you lose your job, but beating yourself up is detrimental to getting on with your job search and your life. As the period of your job search continues, the regular stream of rejections can erode any self-confidence you may have had. This occurs gradually and can cause emotional damage if not immediately addressed.[32]

To take control of your attitude, you must:

- *Take responsibility for your situation and reverse the deterioration of your self-esteem:* Try not to blame yourself or anyone else for your situation. Blame is a negative concept that assumes someone is at fault for poor results and thus should be punished for them. On the other hand, taking responsibility acknowledges that a less-than-desirable outcome has occurred and that you can do something to rectify it. The emphasis shifts from blame to action.
- *Reinforce your self-confidence:* Human nature dictates that your attitude deteriorates in the presence of negative feedback unless there is also present sufficient positive feedback to compensate for it. It is up to you to reinforce your self-confidence in the face of a deluge of negative input. Inside our heads is a voice that talks to us constantly. Unfortunately, much of what it says is negative. In fact, one researcher estimates that as much as 77 percent of what we say to ourselves about ourselves can be classified as self-rejecting.[33] However, you can take charge of that negative voice and refuse to allow it to undermine you. Managing that voice by changing it from a critic that sabotages you to a coach that supports you can prevent you from succumbing to the self-battering that is detrimental to your self-confidence, just when you need self-confidence the most.
- *Distinguish fact from fiction:* According to experts, we all live with our heads full of two kinds of "truths" about ourselves—facts and fictions. Facts are verifiable statements such as "I am 35 years old" and "I graduated from the University of Washington." But we also tell ourselves a lot of fictions. These are both negative and positive judgments we make about ourselves, such as "I am no good with numbers" and "I am not creative," or "I am a numbers person" and "I am quite creative." You may or may not be able to verify these judgments, but even if they are totally fictitious, you act as if they are true. You also tell other people these "truths" and they believe them.[34]
- *Control your thoughts:* Your thoughts may well be the keystone to your attitude. If left uncontrolled, they will take their own course,

which, during a job search, is usually a negative one. You need to learn to listen to yourself. Discipline yourself to recognize the "red flags" that your thoughts provide and immediately take action to redirect them to be more positive.

- *Learn to recognize when you are giving yourself negative signals:* If you hear yourself using the words *always* or *never*, they probably are associated with a negative statement. These are trigger words that can warn you that you are thinking negatively. You must interrupt any negative responses and become aware that your anxiety has distorted what is real. You need to be alert to the fact that rejection and lack of response on the part of potential employers may lead you, little by little, into depression.

- *Take control of your self-talk:* Your self-talk is one of the most significant indications of a declining attitude. This category includes your thoughts about your situation and your future, as well as the feedback you give yourself on any particular event or performance. Control of self-talk is vital to a successful job search because the way you talk to yourself can be both an indicator and an instigator of positive or negative thought. For example, change phrases such as "I can't," "I should," "I want to," and "I'm going to try to." When you say "I can't" to yourself, your brain hears "I accept this limitation in myself." If you say "I should" to yourself, you unconsciously add "but I won't" or "but I can't." When you say "I'm going to try to," you withhold your total commitment. Trying gives you an out. It allows you to procrastinate, to fail. When you say "I want to," you have a wish without a plan. Such statements allow you to wander in a hazy world of fantasy.

  One career counselor suggests the following exercise to take charge of your self-talk and to capture your inner critic. Listen for the voice in your head and write down what it says. Then rewrite the critical self-talk into coach-talk. (See figure 2-5.) Once you have transformed your negative thoughts into written statements of affirmation, reread them frequently and allow yourself to believe what you are saying to yourself. Picture yourself doing what your statement says.[35] Your mind does not like inconsistency. If you tell yourself negative things, you mind helps them come true; if you tell yourself positive things, your mind encourages behaviors that lead to your goals.

Practice Realistic versus Positive Thinking

Although positive thinking is an important part of your job search attitude, if you get carried away and ignore warning signals, it ceases to be beneficial. A more realistic job search attitude is to always look for

Figure 2-5. Transforming Critical Self-Talk into Positive Affirmations

Make your coach's statements:

1. *Positive:* Avoid the word *not,* as in "I do not procrastinate." Somehow, the brain overlooks that word and hears "I do procrastinate." Instead, say "I start tasks quickly."
2. *Personal:* Use the word *I* to begin every statement.
3. *Perfect:* State your thought as if you have already accomplished the change. Give your brain a picture of yourself after you have completed your change.
4. *Passionate:* Use exciting words such as *thrive, love, enthusiastic.* The more emotion your statement generates in you, the faster your mind will find ways to help you accomplish whatever you want to do.

Source: Baber, A. K. *How to Fireproof Your Career: Survival Strategies for Volatile Times.* New York City: Berkley Publishing Group, 1995, pp. 51–52.*

the good but keep in mind some negative and uncontrollable events will probably occur. Just keep reminding yourself that you can deal with these problems as they arise.

It is not necessary, or even possible, to be 100 percent positive all the time. An attempt to accomplish this feat will only place unnecessary pressure on you. Find your natural level of comfort and work on maintaining it. If you are not naturally a confident person, recognize that. Job searching is an emotional roller coaster. Seek only to minimize the ups and downs so you can deal with your search rationally and objectively.

Deal with Some Job Search Realities

There are several realities associated with a job search, all of which can have a negative effect on your attitude. By naming these and acknowledging that they will most likely occur, you can reduce their impact on your attitude. These realities are:

- *You will be rejected far more often than you will be accepted.* You must learn not to take this personally. It is essential that you find some way to deal emotionally with rejection. Remember, prospective employers are not rejecting you as an individual or stating that your qualifications are insufficient. All they are saying is that your background and experience do not make the best fit given the competition and the circumstances surrounding this specific position.
- *Job offers can be rescinded.* Most often, this occurs for reasons beyond your control. Perhaps the hiring individual exceeded his or her authority by making the offer, or political infighting may be the culprit. Numerous factors could have led to the decision that have

nothing to do with your skills. You cannot control the event, but you can control your reactions to it. Do not blame yourself for the event. The important thing is to get back on the job search, and next time keep your options open until you actually start on the job. In this way, you will maintain the momentum of your search.

- *People make decisions slowly.* It is rare to find an employer who is in as much of a hurry as you are to reach a decision. Employers have vacations, travel schedules, and pressing business that will influence the speed with which they make a decision. Your challenge is to appear patient and understanding and to maintain a positive attitude.
- *The salary is rarely as much as you had hoped.* The volatile environment of health care today may increase competition for many jobs, creating a buyer's market and forcing wage rates down. You may have to turn down an offer that is not economically responsible for you to accept. Accepting such an offer may meet your short-term needs at the risk of your long-term financial condition. Do not, however, let your ego persuade you that an offer is beneath you when it is in fact a rational offer. This type of behavior will lead to a long, long job search. To avoid such pitfalls, as you review your financial situation, objectively determine the absolute minimum offer you can accept.

Seven Critical Attributes of an Effective Job Search Attitude

According to Brian Jud, author of *Coping with Unemployment: How to Triumph Over the Negative Emotions of Prolonged Unemployment*, there are seven critical attributes you should maintain to foster an effective job search attitude.[36] Each of these must be monitored and strengthened if they appear to weaken. They will enable you to remain competent, professional, and enthusiastic throughout your job search. These seven attributes are:

1. *Control:* You must exercise control over your attitude, your finances, and your actions during your job search. Controlling your attitude can make you more optimistic and confident; controlling your finances can help you cut back on your expenses so you can extend your deadline for as long as possible; and controlling your actions gives you a sense of mastery as you make decisions for your long-term best interests.
2. *Commitment:* Commitment is your willingness to keep working at your search even when you do not have the self-confidence to do so. If you are committed to your job search, you will continue

contacting people after being rejected or ignored repeatedly, and you will continue calling on people even after you have had a job offer rescinded. Commitment creates action that will in turn bring accomplishment.

3. *Confidence:* Confidence during your job search will require placing trust in yourself and your close allies to eventually find a new position. Although this attribute will take the greatest abuse during your search, you will be more successful, more quickly if you approach your search with a confident, optimistic attitude.

4. *Courage:* Courage is your ability to face adversity; it is the reserve of inner strength you can draw on when the search gets tough. You cannot eliminate fear, but you can face it and control it.

5. *Creativity:* Creativity in your job search will mean you are creating or causing opportunities to happen, bringing offers into being and originating professional ways to gain the prospective employer's attention. Creativity is essential to success in your job search.

6. *Competition:* Competition is the spirit of vying for a prize. In the course of your search, you will obviously compete with others. You also should compete with yourself, always attempting to improve your actions, skills, and whatever it is you need to do to get a job.

7. *Concentration:* When you concentrate on your goals, you direct your attention to the action that will achieve them. Progress during your search will have less to do with speed than with direction. Concentration is the compass that keeps you headed toward your desired outcome.

Putting It All Together: Characteristics of Those Who Prevail

Individuals who are successful in their job search and prevail over the trials of unemployment have many characteristics in common. Psychologist Ann Kaiser Stearns has counseled and studied the unemployed and has identified the common qualities of job loss survivors.[37] These are:

- *Job loss survivors work through the pain of termination and unemployment.* They find emotional release by talking with a confidant, writing in a journal, or engaging in physical activity. They also make an effort to place events into perspective, acknowledging that although job loss is difficult to deal with, many other people suffer in far greater ways. Survivors find encouragement wherever it can be found—in family, friends, books, or special events. They remember, too, to be thankful for all that is still good in their lives.

- *Successful job searchers are proactive.* They make things happen rather than wait for things to happen. They recognize and seize any opportunities that present themselves, even when they are not the exact opportunity being sought. Survivors stay busy through purposeful activity and a daily routine, and live one day at a time, focusing primarily on that day's tasks and concerns. They establish realistic goals and take small attainable steps each day to reach them.
- *Survivors have the courage to ask for help from family, friends, professionals, and support groups.* They also have the courage to change. As frightening as change can be, they are willing to learn new skills and attitudes for a new work environment. They exhibit a belief in hard work and personal integrity, and imagine the future in positive ways.
- *If circumstances assume crisis proportions, survivors develop strategies for coping with the stress and solving specific problems.* They find ways to keep their sense of humor and associate with positive, optimistic people. They are willing to put time and effort into activities that many people avoid, such as working through personal and family problems, becoming healthier through physical activity, aggressively pursuing their job search, and obtaining additional education or skills.

In the final analysis, those who deal successfully with unemployment and job searching acknowledge that life is often unfair, manage their emotions, maintain a positive attitude, and accept responsibility for creating their own future. You can do it, too!

Common Questions and Answers

Following are some common questions that people have about job loss.
The answers provided encapsulate much of the information in this
chapter.

- *I am afraid of my family's response to hearing of my termination. Should
  I delay telling them?* You should not put off telling your immediate
  family about your termination. Withholding this news from them
  will deprive you of a great source of comfort and strength. Further, your family will most likely sense your mood change and
  suspect that something is wrong anyway. Most people, especially
  children, will assume the worst if left to their own imagination
  and interpretation of your changed mood.
- *How do I get over these feelings of hurt and anger toward my former
  employer?* First, your feelings are completely normal. The unemployed experience a cycle of grief and loss, which includes both
  sadness and anger. The best thing you can do is vent your emotions. Find someone, or even several people, you feel comfortable with—and talk, talk, talk. This person can be your spouse, a
  close friend, a member of the clergy, or a professional counselor.
  The more feelings that surface during this venting process, the
  better. Talking about your feelings will keep you from becoming
  overwhelmed by them. You must deal with the past in order to
  prepare yourself to deal with the future.
- *What if my family reacts badly to the news of my termination?* Ideally,
  your family will support and encourage you through this time of
  transition. However, your job loss may be as traumatic (or even
  more so) for your partner or family as it is for you. You must allow
  your family to express their feelings and be reassured that they
  will be taken care of. If your family is struggling with this situation, seek family counseling if necessary and be sure to seek support for yourself outside the family unit. The best protection
  against family stress is family cohesion, support, and communication. Spend time together, listen to one another, and work as
  a team.
- *I am surprised by how difficult my termination has been. Why should
  losing my job be so devastating?* Many of us, in the United States
  in particular, confuse what we do for a living with who we are.
  Consequently, when we lose a job, we feel as though we have
  lost our identity. In the frenzied work world of today, many organizations encourage this kind of thinking by requiring more and
  more hours of their employees each day. There seems to be nothing in our lives except our work. For too many of us, what we

do for a living determines how we view ourselves as well as how others view us. If your sense of self is closely tied to your employment status, unemployment can be surprisingly overwhelming.

- *How can I stop blaming myself for losing my job?* It is natural to doubt your abilities if you lose your job. Continuing to beat yourself up for long, however, is detrimental to getting on with your job search and your life. Instead, try to accept responsibility for dealing with your circumstances. Blame is a negative concept that assumes someone is at fault and should be punished. On the other hand, taking responsibility acknowledges that a less-than-desirable outcome has occurred and you must do something to rectify it.

- *I seem to have lost my desire to work. How can I motivate myself to begin a job search?* Job loss is an experience in bereavement. Before you can be motivated to start your job search, you must be certain you have first dealt with your emotions. Again, vent your thoughts and feelings with a spouse, a trusted friend, or a professional. If your inability to start actively job searching lasts longer than a few weeks, you should consider getting professional counseling.

- *If I don't know how long my job search will take, how can I make sure I have enough money to last the duration?* First, try to avoid imagining financial disaster. Things may not be as bad as you think they are. Next, do a complete financial assessment of your assets, liabilities, income, and expenses. Also, consider seeking the advice of a financial planner to help you decide what to do about credit card debt, how best to utilize severance pay, and how to manage and protect your assets and savings. Finally, create a job search financial plan. Using your assessment and the planner's advice, determine the approximate date that you need to be reemployed without wiping out all your resources. Brainstorm ways to spend less, earn more, and manage your finances better. If your deadline approaches and you remain unemployed, you may have to consider taking a temporary job or a job you do not really want, as a first step.

- *When I have downtime during the job search, I get bored and negative. What should I do?* Two strategies are vital to maintaining your job search: keep busy, and take control of your attitude. Exercise, complete some of those home improvement projects you have been putting off, work in the garden, keep a journal, volunteer your time to those less fortunate, or join a support group. Also, work on controlling your attitude. Take charge of that negative voice inside your head and refuse to allow it to undermine you. Learn to recognize when you are giving yourself negative signals and transform them into positive thoughts. Take control of how you talk to yourself and do not forget to associate with positive rather than pessimistic people.

- *I'm an introvert. Can joining a job search support group really help me?* Even if you do not need the socialization provided by a support group, you can still benefit from participating in one. Support groups provide a means of networking and receiving emotional encouragement and motivational help. Further, attending group meetings will help you keep busy and put some much-needed structure back into your life.
- *How do I deal with all the rejection during the job search?* Try to realize up front that you will be rejected far more times than you will be accepted. You must learn not to take this personally. All a rejection means is that your background and experience do not make the best fit given the competition and the circumstances surrounding the specific position. Frequently, prospective employers are not rejecting you as an individual or even asserting that your qualifications are insufficient. Remember, all it takes is one acceptance!
- *What are the keys to maintaining an effective job search attitude?* You must deal with your emotions and maintain control over your attitude, your finances, and your actions during the job search. Commit to keep working at your search, even when you do not have the self-confidence to do so. Trust in yourself to eventually find a new position. Tap your inner strength and courage when the going gets tough. Continually look for new and creative ways to bring opportunities your way and to gain prospective employers' attention. Always strive to improve your actions and skills. Finally, remain focused on the job search at hand.

References

1. Morin, W. J., and Cabrera, J. C. *Parting Company: How to Survive the Loss of a Job and Find Another Successfully.* San Diego: Harcourt Brace & Company, 1991, pp. 25–29.

2. Morin and Cabrera, pp. 28–29.

3. Baber, A. K. *How to Fireproof Your Career: Survival Strategies for Volatile Times.* New York City: Berkley Publishing Group, 1995, p. 75.

4. Morin and Cabrera, pp. 29–30.

5. Morin and Cabrera, pp. 32–34.

6. Vestal, K. Fired! managing the process. *Journal Of Nursing Administration* 20(6):15, June 1990.

7. Mackey, H. *Sharkproof: Get the Job You Want, Keep the Job You Love in Today's Frenzied Job Market.* New York City: HarperCollins, 1993, pp. 9–10.

8. Vestal.

9. Blouin, A. S., and Brent, N. J. Nurse administrators in job transition: managing the exit. *Journal of Nursing Administration* 22(10):12, Oct. 1992.

10. Blouin and Brent, p. 13.

11. Morin and Cabrera, p. 36.

12. Stearns, A. K. *Living Through Job Loss: Coping with the Emotional Effects of Job Loss and Rebuilding Your Future.* New York City: Simon & Schuster, 1995, p. 24.

13. Stearns, p. 31.

14. Stearns, p. 25.

15. Morin and Cabrera, p. 42.

16. Stearns, p. 39.

17. Baber, p. 82.

18. Stearns, p. 117.

19. Madge, N. Unemployment and its effects on children. *Journal of Child Psychology and Psychiatry* 24(9):311–19, Sept. 1983.

20. Jud, B. *Coping with Unemployment: How to Triumph over the Negative Emotions of Prolonged Unemployment.* Avon, CT: Marketing Directions, 1993, p. 189.

21. Baber, p. 125.

22. Stearns, p. 71.

23. Baber, p. 128.

24. Fagin, L., and Little, M. *The Forsaken Families.* London: Penguin Books, 1984, p. 28.

25. Baber, pp. 54–56.

26. Stearns, p. 87.

27. Stearns, p. 44.

28. Jud, pp. 151–56.

29. Stearns, p. 49.

30. Jud, p. 119.

31. Stearns, p. 64.

32. Jud, p. 15.

33. Baber, pp. 49–50.

34. Baber, pp. 50–51.

35. Baber, pp. 51–54.

36. Jud, p. 21.

37. Stearns, pp. 168–87.

Chapter 3

Organizing and Managing the Job Search

Katherine W. Vestal, PhD, RN

A career in health care is a rich composite of many experiences in the health care arena. The explosion of new health care services and technology has generated enormous opportunities for career growth and expansion. However, searching for a job in the new health care arena is a process that must be carefully thought out and conducted.

This chapter focuses on a variety of issues related to job searching and hiring. These issues have changed significantly over the past decade as the world of work has changed. This job search overview should enable you to pick and choose avenues that make sense for you and should provide practical suggestions to support your journey.

The Changing World of Work

Most of our parents worked for one employer throughout their entire career. They worked at a time when loyalty to the organization was ultimately rewarded with a gold watch and a monthly retirement check. Stories of boredom and sticking it out in order to reach retirement are a part of many a family's lore.

The truth is that this world was not so bad. It supported economic growth, work stability, and an orderly career. In fact, it precluded many people from having to make tough career decisions because career moves generally came to them. Employees were clear about the path upward and expected routine promotions in return for hard work and conformance. At most, disruption might have meant a transfer to another company site, but it was supported by the company move policy and considered the price of success.

In those days, the loss of one's job sent that person to interview for a new job in a somewhat predictable market. Depending on the cycle of the economy, work was usually available, particularly in health care, where explosive growth coupled with cyclical labor shortages to provide new job opportunities.

The Current World of Work

Today, it is difficult to find (if in fact one exists) a health care organization that is not in the process of reinventing itself for the future. Daily reports of mergers, acquisitions, and closures are driving upheavals in the executive and managerial ranks, which in turn lead to new expectations for the staff. Where we work, our relationships with our bosses and peers, and how we are paid are changing rapidly as the workplace itself goes through radical transitions. New concepts such as building teams, empowering employees, and streamlining work have led to a variety of results, including new work flow, new models of leadership and supervision, and new jobs. The expected outcomes focus on improved effectiveness, reduced costs, and the redefinition of services.

Additionally, technology is having a profound effect on how work is done, who does it, and how it is monitored. The processing of information is leading to increased job redefinition and a decade of major work change. Even those who survive the current restructuring may find that the next threat will be related to technology assuming human tasks and to the relentless pressure to develop new technical skills.

The changing process of work and information movement and the revolution in the structure of the health care industry guarantee that we will work in many different jobs—and possibly organizations—during our careers. Most of us probably have experienced this situation already, through either choice or forced circumstances. Coping with frequent upheaval creates anxiety, both personal and organizational, that takes a toll on each of us. Ironically, at the very time we must deal with this anxiety, we are being asked to produce more and to produce it better and faster. Performance excellence is an expectation of every employee, at both executive and staff levels.

Thus, today's world of work is a kaleidoscope of excitement, exhaustion, and sheer terror. Just when we figure it out, it changes. Personal decisions about the future must factor in job security—a security that is difficult, if not impossible to find.

The Future World of Work

If we can imagine the future world of work, we can prepare for it. We can develop a future job mind-set and get busy preparing for the next generation of our career. This future world is already relatively well defined; it is just not universally accepted. In fact, some still hope it will not happen—or at least will not happen to them. However, it will happen; and because of the inevitability of these scenarios, it is imperative that we prepare to compete in the new work world and begin to understand the implications of that world for our new careers.

The future world of work will be defined by a number of characteristics, including:

- Organizations will be flatter, leaner, and more flexible.
- Businesses will be more aggressive in meeting rapidly changing customer demands.
- Tightening and downsizing will continue, and the old jobs and roles will not return.
- New information technology will drive decision making to front-line employees, further eliminating layers of decision makers.
- Job advancement and growth will come from new business units, ventures, or activities needed by the evolving organization.
- Strong pressure for maximum performance and excellence will highlight the star performers and force elimination of the mediocre or poor performers.
- Flexibility and creativity will be valued more than loyalty and endurance. Breadth of knowledge will be critical in adding value.
- New performance management and reward systems will be driven by scorecards and results, at both team and individual levels. Security will be based on value-added results.
- Continuous learning, skill building, and interpersonal success will be required just to maintain a position. The ability to synthesize data, make recommendations, and produce results will be a requirement to advance.

If you accept the premise that the future workplace will be dramatically different, you are ready to explore the implications this world will have on a job search. The old rules for job search no longer apply. If you were to follow them, you probably would not find a job. However, if you develop a search based on the new rules for the new work world, you will have a good likelihood of success.

Finding a good job is difficult task, requiring structure, process, energy, and commitment. This chapter is intended to motivate you to change your old tactics and to try new, innovative, and bold approaches. It is not easy, but it can be done. Commit yourself to a successful search.

The New View of "Job"

The traditional view of a job is that it is a series of activities strung together to produce something. In the past, people were hired to perform specific tasks and then moved from job to job as needs changed. However, this does not hold as true as it once did. In his provocative book, *Job Shift*, W. Bridges hypothesizes that jobs are a social artifact.[1]

He postulates that being employed in the future may not involve a job. This view is worth thinking about as you begin a search for work, because you may want to change your paradigm of what work will be. The concept of job shift is a movement away from "job" to "work that needs doing," which ensures that anyone who can deliver an outcome a customer wants is in a good position. Conversely, anyone who wants to play a traditional role is in a risky position.

Thus, the future world of work will be formed by people who bring specific talents to produce results. The workplace will be an amalgamation of core staff, outsourcing, and contract and project people. Teams will form to accomplish tasks and then disband. Talent will be brought in as needed.

Combining this view with that of the increasingly lean organization, the world of work may take on a whole new concept. What kind of work are you looking for? Will your future work be a tapestry of activities, perhaps with several employers? Will you focus on certain types of projects or leadership and move from opportunity to opportunity?

The point is, if you are making a job transition, you may want to redefine what you are looking for. Interestingly, nurse and other health care executives are alarmed by the declining number of executive jobs. They grieve for the loss of a traditional chief nurse role. Instead, why not celebrate the rapid expansion of the health care continuum and the incredible number of new opportunities to lead clinical services? There is plenty of work to be done; it is just that the way the work is orchestrated may be quite different than it was in the traditional model. Before you launch a job search, make sure you read *Job Shift* and a similar resource by H. Dent titled *Job Shock*.[2]

Finding the Jobs in Health Care

In the old world of health care, it was easy to predict the types and numbers of jobs each organization would have. Today, it is difficult even to define what the health care organization is without extensive research and discussion with people who have an inside track. Because of the day-to-day consolidations and corporate restructures, opportunities arise quickly and often are filled by the surplus of in-house talent. Thus, being in the know is a real challenge. How do you find current information, use it quickly to penetrate a system, and identify opportunities that may exist?

Explore Nontraditional Job Sources and New Opportunities

Job availability tends to be greatest in large, growing organizations and small, start-up enterprises. Both have a need for new talent and are looking for people to join their venture. Exhibiting openness to new directions, high energy, and industry expertise will get you at least to the first round; you can then determine where to go from there.

Other sources of jobs are hidden in competitor agendas, customer demands, and industry changes. Keep up with newsletters, periodicals, and conferences to target potential opportunities. Think through what you might bring to a new venture. Hidden opportunities may have little competition, thus creating a ready market.

Finding hidden opportunities takes diligence and a bit of detective work. Many libraries now have access to computerized databases, newspapers, and annual reports of private and publicly held companies. Organize this up-to-date information in a way that you can reference it throughout your search. Do not forget venture capitalists, who are providing the money for new businesses or for rapid growth, because they influence managerial and executive hires and are always searching for top talent. Newsletters and fund information are other good sources. The world of health care is expanding rapidly, and businesses on the fringe are great places to look. Above all, be creative.

Another source of opportunity is the transference capabilities health care professionals have as a result of their technical knowledge. (See figure 3-1 for a list of employers nurses might consider for alternative job opportunities.) Transference capability is the opportunity to utilize knowledge you have in another area of focus. For example, clinical specialists now find that their technical knowledge can be transferred and applied to the development of new clinical software for the technology industry.

It is useful, too, to scan the literature for "hot jobs" and start-up companies. Because the jobs are often in nontraditional places and organizations, it is essential to use nontraditional resources to find them. The process is not linear; it requires flexibility and perseverance—but it works!

Organize Your Findings and Narrow Your Focus

To dispel the rumors that there are few managerial opportunities in health care, one need only read the literature, contact colleagues, and examine

Figure 3-1.   Alternative Job Opportunities

- Computer services and software
- Biotechnology
- Commercial research
- Pharmaceuticals
- Medical instrumentation manufacturers
- Medical insurance carriers
- Medical equipment and suppliers
- Medical practice management
- Medical facilities management
- Health maintenance organizations
- Outpatient care companies
- Home care companies
- Health care consulting

the changing health care systems. Realistically, the work of providing health care services has not been reduced; if anything, it is increasing with the aging of the population. It is the jobs themselves that are changing.

In many ways, health care professionals are fortunate that the industry is in such chaos. The very chaos that breeds job loss also breeds job growth in the new and emerging components of the industry. Some of these jobs are "hidden," in that they are retitled and transitioned quietly and internally. Others are so new that they are untitled, and job seekers stumble across them during conversation within their network. Still other new jobs are waiting for definition, which you could provide by showing how a new role could add value to the organization.

Organizing a job search approach is a two-step process:

1. *Focus your efforts on the types of organizations you have targeted.* For example, if you are determined to switch careers from acute care to long-term care, it makes sense to concentrate on the long-term care industry. You may find entrée into long-term care through integrated networks that also have acute care facilities, or you may be able to provide solutions for acute care organizations that want to build a long-term care arm. In any event, focus on what you want and narrow your search to best utilize your energy.
2. *Concentrate on targeted organizations and learn about their business in depth.* This way, you will find multiple points of entry as well as valuable information about the business, especially in terms of what opportunities are available and who is responsible for hiring.

Taking the Initiative to Be Prepared

Health care executives today often relate their own fears about where their organizations are going. They graphically describe the prior and emerging organizational changes that will inevitably restructure the workplace. When asked if they fear for their jobs, they usually reply that they do.

Despite the handwriting on the wall, the ability of managers and executives to reposition themselves often is just not there. Usual refrains such as "I'm too busy to think of anything else" and "I'll deal with it when it comes" are counterproductive to the orderly transition of careers.

During a restructuring, your role undoubtedly will change. You will be faced with new requirements, expectations, and selection criteria. So planning in advance and preparing and mobilizing for new opportunities are vitally important, not just to be self-serving (of course you want to be ready to take on whatever arises) but also to help the organization by being ahead of the curve. In fact, it is the dilemma of internal managers not being ready that forces organizations to search externally for candidates to fill new positions. Thus, to be too busy to get ready for future jobs is self-defeating.

It also is an interesting dichotomy that being comfortable in a job breeds complacency. It is not that the work you do is not good but, rather, that by maintaining the status quo (your comfort and the comfort of the organization) you are in fact creating a conflict. By forcing yourself out of this comfort zone and facing challenges and change head-on, you will actually grow and adapt faster. As you push, you create risks and fear— fear of the unknown, to be sure, but also fear that you may not succeed. It is often fear that drives us to action—to remedy the uneasy feelings we have about our own security.

Remember, if you are afraid of losing your job, for whatever reason, there probably is some truth to it. So get busy, prepare yourself now with newer skills, and pay attention to the signals in the organization so that you can take action proactively. Also, any new role or job you assume probably should scare you a bit. There will be things you do not know, faces you cannot read, and adjustments to be made. However, getting use to this need to learn quickly will help you succeed in the transition.

Adjusting to Job Loss

In years past, when someone lost a job, whether through layoff or dismissal, often he or she was viewed as being suspect and thus less likely to be able to recover employment. Today, the stigma of job loss has declined, although a few remnants of the old days remain. Thus, the mantra that it is easier to get a job when you have a job still holds a bit of truth.

However, because many of us will experience an involuntary job transition, it is worth spending a little time framing up that change. C. Hyatt and L. Gottlieb have written an invaluable book called *When Smart People Fail* that should be required reading for anyone who has lost a job.[3] Although, intellectually, many would not view their job loss as a failure, few will fail to experience it that way as they cope day to day.

Among health care professionals, winning and losing are daily occurrences. Patients live, patients die. Despite our best efforts, it is impossible to control everything, and disappointments occur. Job loss is the same. Despite your best efforts, your long days, your unquestionable loyalty to the organization, you are now out—unwanted and unappreciated. You suffer hurt, disappointment, and sadness. Even those who receive good severance packages, early retirement, or transition assistance find the loss immeasurable. Thus, in a sense, we all deal with failure, real or imagined.

The important messages in Hyatt and Gottlieb's book are these:[4]

- *Figure out what happened, because it can become a learning experience to help you in the future.* Was it a lack of team participation or of sensitivity to others? Was it political naïveté about office politics? Was it a lack of contemporary skills needed for the future? Was it the perception of being obstinate or wed to the past? Or was it simply a surplus of people? Be honest with yourself; it was something.
- *Reinterpret your story.* If you leave your job feeling powerless, angry, or depressed, you are unlikely to be a great candidate for a new job. So you must find a way to reinterpret your experience in a context that prepares you to move forward. Within the reality of truth, there are ways to reframe your experience to regain the control and self-worth to move on. Find a way to visualize job loss as a win so that you can enter the marketplace with enthusiasm.
- *Relabel yourself.* When you are unemployed, how do you answer the dreaded question: "What do you do?" To respond "I'm an unemployed nurse" or "I'm a laid-off executive" is a demoralizing way to begin a conversation. Relabeling your experience may require you to say "I'm a health care executive making a transition from hospitals to the growth side of the industry—home care." This is a career change, not just a job change. So change your language, change your label, become an explorer who exudes optimism and energy.
- *Get unstuck, expand your choices.* This message is inherent in all career books, but critical for health care professionals. An industry in chaos requires new options, both seeing and pursuing them. Choices expand as your talents expand, and you become open to "wild ideas." Getting unstuck is personal; expanding choices is professional.
- *Establish transitional steps.* Experiencing job loss is not for the faint of heart. It requires a plan to navigate the transition. Uncluttering your mind, making financial plans, finding a support group, and learning to ask for help all become a part of surviving a career transition. Nurses, and nurse executives in particular, are terrible at asking for help. After all, are we not the ones to provide help and support? This is a time when you need to find others to help you!

It is common to find professionals in career transition who are depressed, angry, and caught in a vicious cycle of poor self-worth. These individuals attempt to find jobs, only to be rejected again and again. Often the rejection is a result of their own presentation—low energy, distrustful, bitter. Putting some of this behind you is essential to moving forward. Being able to diagnose the situation, plan alternatives, and reshape the events of the transition are central to finding new opportunities.

The Successful Job Search

To compete successfully in today's job market, you must make the transition from a self-focused mind-set to a customer-focused mind-set. If you enter into a search asking "What can this job do for me?" your approach is likely to yield many dead ends. However, by asking "What role can I fill that will add value to the customers of this organization?" you will be well on your way to success.

One of the main differences in the second approach is that the work that needs to be done may not resemble the "job" you want. In fact, the concept of job as we know it may be becoming obsolete. This is an important concept to comprehend, because it can enable you to greatly broaden your thinking about potential work opportunities as you look to the future.

There are at least two types of people in the work world—those who wait for success, and those who go out and get it. Luck has very little to do with success these days. Most people are working hard to succeed and getting noticed for their contributions.

In a world where organizations are downsizing and changing, there is a constant search for the best talent. After all, if there are fewer managers and staff, the ones who are there had better be good! So each round of change provides an opportunity to select and reselect the best.

Thus, it is imperative that you be noticed for your talents. The things you contribute that add value to the organization must be highlighted. That way, whether you are selected for a role internally or search externally, word that you have clear and important talents will have preceded you. You may think it is the responsibility of others to notice how good you are, but in reality, it is your responsibility to ensure that you are noticed.

Getting noticed in today's chaotic workplace requires that you:

- *Make a plan:* A plan for getting noticed should be related to your professional goals and what you are striving for. You must be able to share your plan with others—leaders, managers, and mentors—so that they can help you and provide feedback. A thorough plan, well executed, will ensure that you are noticed!
- *Getting results:* Nothing speaks louder than results. If you have reduced a cost, improved a clinical outcome, or made a difference

in the workplace, you must make others aware of what you have accomplished. (Above all, use the term *result, outcome,* or *critical success factor.*) For example, write a one-page results report for the executives, notify the company newsletter, or report the result to the committee responsible for outcomes related to your work. While it may seem a routine part of your job to produce good outcomes, it is especially important for your career that others notice that you are making a difference.

- *Market yourself:* If you added value to the organization by ensuring that a strategic goal was accomplished, that is important. Learn to use communication avenues within the organization, including newletters, bulletin boards, and E-mail, as well as through professional societies and local groups, to enhance your professional image both inside and outside of your organization. By elevating your professional profile, you will build linkages and relationships that may be critical to your future job network.

Develop a Way to Manage Your Search

A job search is a series of emotional highs and lows tied together by phone calls, letters, and interviews. If it were possible to stand back and watch from a distance, you would see a fascinating dance of many tempos and intensity. Unfortunately, when you are the one searching for a job, the view from the inside is much more fragile. The search process is at best a roller-coaster ride—the highest of highs, the lowest of lows, and a lot of twists and turns along the way.

You must consider how you will manage yourself through the process. How will you deal with the emotional extremes and even out the process? If you cannot find a way to do that, you may be interviewing for a great position when you are low.

A few practical suggestions may help you frame up your approach to self-management:

- *Accept that a roller-coaster ride is inevitable.* Having done this, simply monitor your progress and seek support where needed. For instance, develop a support group of family or colleagues whom you can talk to when you are low. It is important to work through a low period. People who have been through a similar experience may be most helpful. If you feel your low periods are too often or too intense, seek professional counseling.
- *Assemble a short list of professional colleagues who will support you throughout the search.* When you have been fired or laid off, sometimes many of the people you thought were friends will turn out to be only work-related acquaintances and suddenly will disappear

from your life. Some will be afraid to call you because they fear retribution at work; others simply do not know what to say. A few will call weekly, send you leads, help you with contacts, and be there to celebrate the new job. This short list of supporters is incredibly important and will require your attention later. Your disappointment with the others is a personal challenge.

- *Get busy and stay busy with your search.* You must work hard at a search, day in and day out. If you treat it as a hobby, to be done when time allows, you will not give it enough effort to move quickly. Therefore, treat your search as a job. If you have too many distractions at home or at work, find a place to go where you can concentrate, use a phone, and relentlessly pursue leads.

A lot of good can come out of a job search. You will learn a lot about yourself and others. You will find incredibly interesting opportunities, and you will likely agonize over declining an offer because it is too far off your plan. You also will happily celebrate when your goal is met.

Learn How to Master Success

The definition of a successful job search is "getting what you want," which is a very different outcome from "getting a job." In fact, during a search you will likely interview for several types of roles, with multiple employers, and thus the permutations of results are endless.

There are three important steps involved:

1. Determine what you want in a job.
2. As you interview, identify the issues that relate to your plan.
3. Determine how you will measure your successes and maintain the positive momentum of your search.

Determine What You Want in a Job

This is a personal assessment. What are your thoughts about the perfect job? What do you want? You may want to sketch out a chart that structures your thoughts and what you might contribute to an organization.

As You Interview, Identify the Issues That Relate to Your Plan

If you take the time to write out the information, the decisions to be made become clearer. Without a plan, emotion prevails and you may take a job that has little relevance to your needs. Therefore, assume you will need to conduct your job search from basically a clean sheet of paper. You can make any decision you want, determine your interests, and then proceed with finding a new job. Your own realities can be factored in as needed, but at least an ideal process can be formulated.

As has already been discussed, in many ways looking for a job is in itself a full-time job. First, you must get your head in it and stay focused in order to reach your goal. Second, once you set a series of events into motion, you must be prepared to follow through. It does no good to network, for example, if you do not have time to return calls or generate interest before you have taken the time to update your resume. Therefore, to make the most of a search, you must make it a high priority in your life.

Determine How You Will Measure Your Successes and Maintain the Positive Momentum of Your Search

A successful job search is a series of little wins. If your only line of sight is on *the job,* you will miss the successes you have along the way. So it is important to think about milestones and indicators that reinforce your process. There are two ways to do this:

1. Look at the job transition itself:
   * How was the decision made to change jobs?
   * Did you manage the process well from the organization's view?
   * Were you able to transition professionally and not burn bridges?
   * Did you get closure with the decision?
   * Do you feel good about how you handled the situation?
2. Set up indicators that offer you positive feedback:
   * Did I establish a good plan for the process?
   * Am I working the plan aggressively?
   * Are people returning my calls?
   * Do my materials look professional?

The list can be endless, but the point is simple: You must find measures of success to feed the momentum of a search. When there are setbacks, the next success is critical. If you look at the search process as a series of wins, you can track your progress. If you focus only on the end product, you may be derailed early on. So celebrate each win, pat yourself on the back, and keep moving forward.

Make a Few Fundamental Decisions

A few fundamental decisions must be made in order to frame up your options. Although not an exhaustive list, the following questions should be considered:

- By when do I want to have a new job?
- When will I start the process?
- Where do I want to live?
- Am I willing to move?
- What type of work do I most want to do?
- Is job prestige important to me?
- What makes me happy in a job?
- What undeveloped interests do I have?
- Do I want a structured or unstructured job?
- Am I project oriented or daily process oriented?
- Do I want a staff or line role?
- Am I a leader or a follower?
- Am I a builder or a maintainer?
- What motivates me?
- What about money? title? work hours?
- What kind of boss do I want?

You must consider these questions before beginning a job search. It would be a little odd to have a search firm ask whether you would relocate only to have you respond that you have not thought about it. You must think about it early, make a decision, and work within the parameters of that decision. As you search, you may modify those parameters, but it is important to begin with a concrete position.

A case example may be helpful. Recently, a nurse executive was transferred out of her job. Although her transition was involuntary, she was given a 9-month severance package. In thinking about her next job, she was adamant about not wanting to go into a similar executive role in a hospital. Therefore, she declined all opportunities to interview for hospital-based nurse executive roles and, instead, focused all her efforts on nontraditional roles in health care, especially in the managed care arena. Because she was willing to relocate, she identified a clear picture to others who could help her and narrowed her search by excluding some options and staying focused on her plan. No doubt, she will be successful in finding the job she desires. Her likelihood of success is enhanced by having in place a decisive search plan.

The Search Process

The search for a new job has two distinct components: the process (how you orchestrate the many details of the initiative), and the product (the job you want). Of the two, the hardest to manage is the process, which involves myriad details. Yet, if you manage the process well, the result—a job—will follow. There are jobs, and then there are jobs you want. A well-thought-out and well-executed process will lead you to the jobs, after which you can make decisions about your interest. Thus, the work is really about the journey. When people appear to be having an extremely difficult time finding a job, often it is because they either are focused too narrowly, have limited the process to too few options, or do not follow through on the details.

It probably is accurate to say that most job searches are won or lost by the way the search is conducted. The job search consists of three phases:

1. *Get ready.* There are an amazing number of things to do in order to launch a job search. It is best to organize these at the beginning of the search; otherwise, rather than going forward, you will be returning constantly to preparation activities.
2. *Work the plan.* This phase makes use of the preparation and planning, and forces you to stay focused on the process and to follow through.
3. *Make it happen.* During this phase the leads are coming in, the interviews are scheduled, and decisions are to be made.

Phase 1. Get Ready

Many of the activities needed to initiate a job search have been discussed previously; they are reviewed here to help you organize your search process.

Step 1. Clarify What You Want

In starting your search process, you must first determine what you want in a job. If your personal preferences are not clear, your outcomes will be defined by someone else and may not meet your needs. Consider these questions:

- What are my career and/or job goals?
- What options do I have?
- What is my timing for finding a job?

It is helpful to talk these questions over with family or friends to gain a clear understanding of what you want and to help you articulate those desires as you search for a job. If you do not know what you want, you will waste the time of those you contact. During this process, you also may find that you need to take more time to develop a career plan that clarifies the skills you need to meet your targeted goals. (See table 3-1.)

Table 3-1. Getting Clarity about What You Want in a Job

What I Want in a Job	Skills Needed	What the Job Offered
Responsibility	• Managerial/executive	•
Measurable and solid value	• Statistical measurement • Marketing/sales • Analytical thinking	•
Status and visibility	• Presentation skills • Executive presence	•
Creativity	• New approaches/ open mind	•
Working with talented people, especially the boss	• Selection • Collegial • Team	•
Chance to grow with the organization	• Increased knowledge of managed care • Network/negotiation skills	•
Learn new things	• Environmental scanning • Technology-based tools	•
Global experience	• Multicultural • International business	•

Step 2. Establish a Personal Infrastructure for Your Job Search

Because a job search is a process of selling yourself, it requires a lot of energy and commitment. To cope with the ups and downs of the process, it is helpful to weave a "cocoon" of support around you in order to keep you centered. Several issues are important to address:

- *Outplacement services:* If you were fortunate enough to receive outplacement assistance from your former employer, be sure you understand the breadth and depth of services provided. An outplacement service is neither a search firm nor a placement firm but, rather, a support system that aids your search by providing an office site to work out of and by advising you on all aspects of planning, interviewing, and conducting a search. Often it also provides career testing and counseling.
- *Financial advice:* Get your financial house in order to free you for your job search. (See chapter 2.) It is advisable to seek financial counseling if you are out of work and need to manage your money more efficiently. Often job seekers wait too long, spend too much energy worrying, and become distracted from the search.

- *Establish personal support systems:* Talk with those close to you about the process you are embarking on and let them know how they can help. Be sure they know when you need someone to listen to you. Because professionals going through job loss tend to become more and more isolated as time goes on, which can lead to low morale and depression, it is important to establish these links early.
- *Develop a professional support system:* Determine a few professional colleagues who can listen and give you advice. It is critical to be able to talk over job options as they arise with someone who knows you. You cannot use headhunters to do this because they are representing the client who is hiring. However, do not deal with personal angst with members of your network or with professionals associated with your search. Select a small "club" of people who have the breadth of experience and contacts necessary to help you. These same people can help you prepare for interviews and give you feedback on your search process.

Step 3. Develop the Tools for Your Search

The major tools to develop initially are a cover letter, a resume, and an information-tracking guide to organize your thoughts. You also will need to be able to use technology to your advantage, so you may need to take computer classes to learn how to use the Internet and how to access data.

- *The cover letter:* The cover letter is a stepping stone to getting your resume noticed. It is a tool to gain entry into the system. A cover letter that generates interest is 5 percent of the task of getting an interview; the other 95 percent is follow-up. A good cover letter contains:
  - No more than three paragraphs, totaling less than one page (otherwise it will not be read).
  - Recognition that you understand the organization and know why you want to pursue a job there. If possible, reference a current person in the organization.
  - A description of other roles you are interested in.
  - Two or three ways you would add value to the organization (not what you want but how you can help the organization).
    The cover letter in figure 3-2 successfully meets those criteria. The letter must be specific enough to get attention, yet brief enough to survive perusal. If it appears to be nonspecific or mass mailed, it almost certainly will not be considered. Therefore, do your homework and be clear about what you want. Also, do not use the cover letter to rehash your resume; the two are separate elements.

Figure 3-2.　Sample Cover Letter

August 28, 1996

Katherine W. Vestal, Ph.D.
Vice President and Managing Director, Healthcare Consulting Services
Hay Group, Inc.
12801 N. Central Expressway, Suite 1000
Dallas, Texas 75243

Dear Dr. Vestal:

Congratulations on the superb job your consulting firm just completed in designing an integrated delivery system for St. Joseph Health System. The newspaper coverage was extremely positive.

I recently spoke to one of your partners, Deborah Proctor, about the possibility of joining your consulting group. As you begin to assist St. Joseph with implementing its plan, and others as well, my experience in physician integration and process design would be an asset to your team.

As a health care executive for University Hospital and Health System, I accomplished the following:

- Developed a physician network that resulted in a 20 percent growth in annual business
- Created new work processes to reduce costs by 28 percent and to improve patient satisfaction scores by 14 percent
- Designed and initiated a team-based organizational structure that supported a move to a network culture

I would be most interested in understanding what you are looking for in terms of qualifications for your new hires, and what your time frames are for hiring in your organization. I will call your office to set up a time when we can talk.

Thank you for your assistance.

Warm regards,

C. J. Bolster

- *The resume:* Customize your resume. Thanks to computerization, this is a relatively easy process. In fact, if you are carefully targeting hiring managers, you should be able to customize both the cover letter and your resume. Unfortunately, most resumes are filed with little consideration because either they were too hard to get through or too general, or someone was too busy to read them, especially if there are no active searches under way.

  Often timing is everything. This means you need both a preliminary plan to target the job being hired for and a follow-up plan to ensure your resume was noticed. Because organizations now can scan resumes and create resume databases based on specific skills or characteristics, the content of your resume is critical. Eliminate the fluff, and include only pertinent experience and specific results or accomplishments.

  A great resume is tailored to highlight the needs the organization is searching for. It clearly states your career goals, career accomplishments (increased revenue by x percent, decreased costs by y percent, improved quality by z percent, and so on), special awards or recognition, key player roles, and education/preparation. Because of the key phrases of resume databases, you also should determine buzzwords pertaining to the industry and carefully use them. Figure 3-3 is an example of an effective resume.

  Obviously, the longer your career and the more impressive your contributions, the more substantial your resume will be. There is no page limit; just be sure the content is meaningful and reflects your experience in the industry. There is no excuse for misrepresenting your achievements, so do not even consider doing so. There are so many checks and balances in job searches these days that anything less than full disclosure would be foolhardy.

  Finally, keep your resume simple. It should not be too long, difficult to read, or too trendy. Consult several software packages and decide to approach this issue.

- *Information-tracking guide:* As a part of keeping up with massive quantities of information, you should develop a tracking system to use throughout the search process. Following are three types of tracking systems:

  - *Overall plan of action:* Lay out your plan to make contacts and follow up. You should be aggressive. If you work 40 hours a week on your search, for example, you probably will contact at least 25 people a week and will have substantive conversations with 8 of them. You also may want to research up to three potential target organizations a week. If your goal is to develop a network of 100 people, you will need to call three times that number. These examples begin to define the magnitude of a search.

Figure 3-3. Sample Resume

Denise Allen
2020 East Main
Los Angeles, California 60320
(213) 555-4511

Career Objective

A midlevel health care position in a full-service, global practice focused on the development of integrated delivery systems.

Experience

St. Elsewhere   1992–Present
Los Angeles, California
Manager, Managed Care Accounts

- Developed new sales and marketing campaign that resulted in a 35% increase in revenue
- Established key team roles among all managed care providers in the southern California market
- Successfully negotiated $200 million in contracts
- Reduced disenrollment by 8% in one year

Texas General   1988–1992
Blue Skies, Texas
Manager, Women's Services

- Redesigned and expanded women's service line to provide a full continuum of care
- Improved market share by 6% in one year, 8% in year two, and currently steady at 48% of the total market
- Recruited three OB-Gyn physicians and remodeled office space for practice
- Developed marketing and promotional strategies to improve community perception of care
- Developed and published a report card of services for the women's service

United Hospital   1983–1988
Atlanta, Georgia
Staff Nurse

- Provided clinical care and services in the women's center, medical ICU, and emergency department
- Developed the shared governance model for nursing with a team of staff
- Initiated a departmental newsletter to keep staff up to date
- Participated in a clinical reengineering process to reduce the length of stay and cost per case by 10%

(Continued on next page)

Figure 3-3.   (Continued)

Denise Allen

Special Qualifications

- Computer competent on a variety of software packages
- Noted for creativity and collaboration
- Focused on results and organizational success
- Published in numerous professional publications

Education

- BSN, Texas Christian University
- MS/MBA, Emory University
- Ph.D. in progress (organizational development), UCLA

References upon Request

A major change requires a major search. For a minor change, or a part-time job, the investment in time may be less, but the quality of the results is still determined by the quality of the search process.

— *Contact report:* You will want to develop a contact data sheet that banks information, referrals, and follow-up for each targeted organization. (See table 3-2.) Again, use a software contact reporting system that allows you to constantly update and review information.

— *Progress report:* If you are working your plan closely, you can accurately track your progress week by week — goals, contacts, and actual time involved. Usually, people keep track of phone calls made for information, calls made to hiring managers, letters and resumes sent, phone interviews/screens, and face-to-face interviews. It is often surprising how much you forget if you do not keep a written record. We all overestimate, underestimate, or simply omit, so keep a progress report, celebrate your efforts, and get back on track if you digress.

The elements of a search are really very basic: a good plan, support, and the appropriate tools. Once these are in place and you are confident of their quality, you are ready to proceed. Now you simply put the plant to work — rigorously, relentlessly, and relevantly.

Phase 2. Work the Plan

Working your plan takes discipline, tenacity, and a lot of hard work. Treat it as a full-time job. You have experience working 50 to 60 hours a week, and this search should feel the same.

There are basically two components of action. The first is to get information — the process of networking (that is, gathering information about jobs, organizations, and contacts). The basic purpose of a network is to share information. The second component is to develop leads from this information. During this phase you take useful and timely information, and craft it into actions that result in direct job leads.

Again, entire books have been written on developing and using networks, so the information provided here is meant to give you only a general overview. You can seek more in-depth information if necessary, in general books on career, job search, and personal growth.

Getting Information

Getting information today is a real hunting process. There are so many sources of information and systems for getting to it that it often appears

Table 3-2. Information-Tracking Guide

Contact	Contact #1	Contact #2	Contact #3	Special Notes
Adams, Sue Senior VP University Health Systems 12121 Elm St. St. Elsewhere, TX 214/902-4888	6/15/96 call back 6/17, 2 p.m.	6/17—called Agreed to send letter and resume 6/17		Referred by Tom Raine
Vestal, Kathie Partner Hay Group, Inc. 12801 N. Central Expy. Suite 1000 Dallas, TX 75243 214/934-6836	6/18/96 Sent thank- you note 6/18			Referred to Sam Smith and Sue Walker
Thomas, John VP, HR St. Joseph Health System 1157 Main St. Ft. Worth, TX 76219 817/350-3300	6/18/96 Sent resume			Responding to job ad

overwhelming. Get organized, use your tracking systems to keep up with what you find, and use one or more of the following resources:

- *Libraries:* Libraries contain enormous amounts of information, including books, electronic databases, journals, newspapers, and periodicals. The good news is that much of the information is free and experts are available to help you find it. On the other hand, the probability is somewhat low that newspaper or journal ads will lead to much. Generally, they get so many responses that it is difficult to be noticed.
- *Professional associations:* Professional associations often maintain job search banks for their members. The American Organization for Nurse Executives and the American College of Healthcare Executives list jobs, and individuals can review positions and apply if interested. Though only a small component of the market, associations may be useful for learning about specific trends and salary information. Although associations try to be supportive of their members, in reality, they are primarily an information resource.
- *Local business and community organizations:* Never underestimate contacts from the chambers of commerce, local business coalitions, community organizations, and professional peers in other industries. This personal part of your network is valuable and relatively easy to access. This is especially true if you are an active member of community organizations and know the people.
- *Employment services:* Be careful to distinguish between employment services that charge a fee to help find leads from those working on behalf of employers. An employment service is expensive, rarely has an adequate job base, and only furnishes leads for follow-up. It is an expensive resource, so check it out carefully.
- *Professional search firms:* These firms exist to help employers define jobs, find candidates, and fill the roles. There are many that specialize in health care. They are paid by employers on either a contingency basis (usually 25 to 30 percent of the first year's salary) or a retained basis (a specified amount of money per month for the duration of the search process). They want to find outstanding candidates who will be successful in the job, so they work hard to source possible applicants, screen them, and present a slate of candidates to the employer. Knowing search professionals (often called headhunters) is extremely valuable. You can call them to discuss possible jobs and get general information. However, if the headhunter does not know you or if you are not referred by someone he or she knows, the chance that he or she will entertain your resume is slight. In fact, headhunters are busy too, and are likely to concentrate on employed individuals who surfaced during their

network process. One big lesson to be learned is that building relationships with health care search experts is a career network issue.
Start early and return phone calls!
- *A people network:* The professional grapevine is active, and
  knowledge of job openings, restructuring, and new services is
  usually "on the drums" long before it ever hits the want ads. In
  addition, such jobs are usually filled through recommendations
  to others. Therefore, it is critical to quickly build a web of people
  who will share information with you. Simply telephoning people you know to get their input, advice, or referrals will in turn
  lead to additional referrals. It is important that your purpose be
  to find information. If you try to pressure people into helping you
  find a job, they will disappear into the "no-phone zone." The purpose of your call should be to:
  - Ask a consultant if he or she would be willing to spend a few
    minutes talking to you about consulting
  - Ask a home care administrator if he or she would talk you
    through the best ways to transition to home care
  - Talk to an insurance company about how it is using nurses in
    case management
  - Make similar informational requests of a variety of people who
    can provide information
     As you gather information, leads will surface and you can
  often determine who the hiring manager is. This is important
  because once you know who is making the hiring decisions, you
  can talk to, and correspond directly with, that person and create
  a clear line of sight for your resume. You may even ask a credible
  colleague who knows the hiring manager to write or call on your
  behalf. Once personally recommended, you may get special consideration, a second look, or a prioritized resume to be forwarded
  to the search firm.

One word of advice: Life is full of quid pro quos, so as you impose
on people's time and energy, remember there will come a time when
you can return the favor. Never forget a debt, no matter how minor. Also,
if you have spent your career not returning headhunters' phone calls,
treating consultants and other providers with contempt, or simply not
being involved professionally, you may find your ability to network with
others to be difficult. Conversely, by being helpful and supportive to
others, your professional network will be eager to help you.

Developing Leads

Leads are connections to real jobs or career opportunities. Getting leads
is key to making contact with the hiring manager or search executive,
or at least getting your name on his or her radar screen.

However, effectively pursuing leads and turning them into interviews requires careful planning. For starters, be clear that any contact you have focuses on what the organization needs and how you might help it meet its needs. Do not fall into the old "me-me-me" two-minute script that ignores the organization. You will want to learn the organization's challenges and upcoming changes so that you can suggest how you would add value.

This is where your initial self-review, skills inventory, and career interest work will come into play. You will be converting your strengths and experiences into what the organization wants. You must show the characteristics it is interested in. The organization also may get to judge your tenacity and persistence as you undoubtedly make many calls to ultimately connect with it.

To do this, you must view yourself as a valuable asset, not a pest. You frequently will be working through secretaries or receptionists, so you will need to speak confidently and succinctly. You also get much better responses if you make it clear you are just looking for information; it keeps you from being transferred or from creating pressure for a job. Explain when and where you will be available for a return call or, ideally, schedule a time with the person you hope to talk with.

Following are additional suggestions:

- *Rehearse using voice mail.* Keep your message succinct and ask for a response. As annoying as the endless voice mail circle can be, you must use it to your advantage. For instance, it is often possible to reach the voice mail of executives directly if you call on off hours or weekends. Sometimes, by calling early or late, you may actually reach the executive directly.

    Of course, voice mail works both ways. Be sure your message is professional and clear about how you can be reached. In fact, it may be a good investment to use a more professional alternative to your home answering machine, such as a professional answering service.

- *Send mailings.* You also may want to correspond by mail with your key target organizations. You can drop the chief executive officer a note as a follow-up to a good journal article, relate having met one of his or her peers, or simply send your cover letter and resume. Usually, you want to indicate the follow-up you want in the letter and then make it happen. If, for example, you say you will call, do so. Then call back and call back again. Often such follow-up and persistence will get the results you want.

- *Use the Internet.* You may get occasional leads from the Internet. This relatively new resource allows you to learn about the organizations you want to contact, to chat with others, and to pick up information that may turn into a viable lead. These days, the ability to surf the net is almost a must!

- *Use your mentors/coaches wisely.* Once you have picked their brains, reviewed their Rolodex, and determined their sphere of influence, you can use your mentors/coaches as sounding boards. Their feedback is supportive both personally and professionally. You should keep them informed and involved. Let them know about your leads, review your contacts with them, and leave them messages about your progress. Because they are no doubt busy people, you must do the work to keep them connected to your job search.

  Likewise, you should know when to ask them for advice. If your calls are constantly rebuffed, review your approach with your mentors for feedback. If you get no response to your targeted mailings, ask them to evaluate your materials. If you have a coach, let him or her give you feedback on your strengths and your job search issues.

Clearly, to get leads you must think expansively. This is no time to pull into a shell, vow to "do it yourself," or fight the demons of professional embarrassment. Make use of others and then someday do the same for them.

Phase 3. Make It Happen

In this phase, the leads you have so carefully cultivated begin to bear fruit. First, there will be telephone screens and interviews, then on-site interviews with individuals and teams, and finally an interview with the hiring executive. There also may be developmental assessments, presentations, or other submissions of materials. Eventually, there may be an offer.

Having reached this point after your own screening and careful deliberation, you probably are ready to get on with it. However, you now are entering the organizational bureaucracy of hiring—the hurry-up-and-wait phase with the attendant difficulties of contacting interviewers and working around multiple schedules. This process is what makes even a straightforward search a time-consuming "slow dance." Your time frame may be to make a decision and move on, but the organization's may be to take its time before eventually making a decision. If your schedules are in serious conflict, this ultimately may preclude a deal. However, a thorough understanding of the final hiring process may help you navigate this process successfully.

The Initial Screenings

The initial resume screening is intended to identify a first cut of candidates. Resumes that make the cut are reviewed for experience, results, and organizational fit. Keep in mind that this first review is done by the hiring sponsor. If you mailed your resume to a box number in a newspaper ad, the reviewer is likely to be a clerk or a computer. If you mailed it to a human resources department, it may be reviewed by a personnel recruiter or the human resource manager. If the resume went to a search firm with no particular recruiter identified, it probably will go in the file. If the resume was requested by a recruiter, he or she probably will review it seriously, make the resume cuts, and present the top candidates to the employer.

Unfortunately, applicants who fail to make the cut are seldom notified and frequently spend a lot of time on follow-up. Therefore, it is important to keep up with each of your serious pursuits, using your tracking system and diligent follow-up. You may want to call the screening person for feedback. Ask what you need to do to improve your materials. Was some vital piece of information missing? Was the evidence of your accomplishments too brief? Was your resume too long, too short, too far from the job description? Occasionally, you will find someone who will give you valuable feedback so that you can clarify issues enough to get back on the list!

Usually, a second screening is used to narrow the candidates to a few who will be interviewed. Typically, the hiring sponsor begins with a phone interview. It is easy to underestimate the importance of this interview. Because the hiring sponsor calls you at home, often impromptu, you may be in a situation that is distracting or noisy. If so, say so, and reschedule the interview for a time when you can be prepared. Then treat this phone appointment as a critical meeting. Have your scripts, resume, and written examples of key accomplishments in front of you. Be professional, engaging, and, at the same time, a good listener. Remember, a decision to go forward will take place at the end of this call. If the interviewer is a professional search executive, be prepared for a lengthy (several hours sometimes) in-depth review of your life, professional career, and goals. Also recognize that everything you say is in the record and will likely be circulated in a summarized written form, so choose your words carefully.

You may have multiple phone interviews. Again, treat each one as a formal meeting. Be consistent in your responses and listen for the real meaning of the questions. Also, remember that these initial conversations usually never touch on pay or specific rewards of the job. It is better not to ask until you are much further along. If they really want you, they eventually will work out the details to your satisfaction.

On-Site Interviews

In today's work world, no organization wants to make a hiring mistake for a key executive or manager. To ensure success, organizations have you interviewed by many people so that they can share their views and, ultimately, the hiring responsibility. Therefore, be prepared for a hectic interview schedule.

It also is common to have search committees or teams interview you in a group. If you have not done a lot of group interviews, you should rehearse and find a way to approach it in a relaxed way. Often it is somewhat confusing and unnerving to be pummeled with questions in an intense group atmosphere. Surprisingly, you may find that committee members talk more among themselves than they do to you. When being interviewed, it is helpful to:

- Be informed about the organization and its needs.
- Be enthusiastic and positive.
- Ask questions in a proactive manner rather than waiting to be asked if you have questions.
- Keep your responses short, to the point, and clear.
- Measure your responses carefully, especially if you are likely to be perceived as aggressive or arrogant. Your confidence may be open to a lot of interpretation.

Keep in mind, too, that there are a limited number of questions to be asked and your responses should be somewhat consistent. You can prepare your answers by thinking ahead about typical questions such as:

- What do you know about our organization?
- Why were you laid off?
- Why did you leave your last organization?
- What can you bring to us?
- How would you describe your management style?
- What is your experience with unions?
- What are your goals/ambitions?
- Give examples of successful changes that you led.
- What would your detractors say about you?
- What do you see as the biggest challenge of this job?

People love "war stories" and examples, so include these in your answers, describing what you have experienced that lends credibility to your presentation. It also is appropriate to ask the interviewers questions. For example:

- What is your understanding of this job?
- Why is this job being created?
- Are there political challenges to its success?
- What are the most important results needed? When?
- What is the response of the organization to newcomers?

In asking such questions, candidates sometimes find that the senior people in the organization have different descriptions and expectations of a job. Such diversity in responses should be a red flag for you. Obviously, the answers need clarification before you can determine what you are walking into. The risk of taking a poorly defined job may be limited if it is across the street from your old job; but if you will be required to uproot your family, move across country, and make other life changes, the price of that risk goes up exponentially.

At the end of the second round of interviews, the candidate list is usually cut to one to three finalists who again are interviewed by the hiring executive. At that point, you need to learn as much as you can about your potential new boss. Is there good chemistry, mutual trust, stability, and a history of people liking to work for him or her? There will be substantial data for you, both objective and subjective. Just as the organization may choose you, you have to choose it. A large percentage of people who lose their jobs are fired because they do not have a good relationship with their boss, so if you get "bad vibes," or the atmosphere feels competitive, or reportedly the boss is on tenuous ground, be wary when making your decision.[5]

In the final analysis, you should be able to answer the following questions enthusiastically:

- Is this job what I want to do?
- Is the boss someone I want to work with?
- Is the team a group I can work with?
- Is this city where I want to live?
- Is this opportunity constructed right for me?
- What will I learn in this role? How will it enrich my career?

If you can address these issues enthusiastically, you are ready to negotiate your deal, once they select you. The specifics of how you might construct your package can be found in the chapter 4.

Following are a few practical hints to remember for your interviews and contacts with potential or hiring organizations:

- Do not talk too much, but make every word count.
- Use the conversations to reinforce your resume and your accomplishments.
- Understand the organization's needs before you try to sell yourself.
- Know as much as possible about the organization. Data and information are everywhere. Find them.
- Be positive about your former jobs and employers. Find good things to say.

- Do not become argumentative or defensive, even when baited.
- Be clear who the hiring manager is.
- Do not insult the interviewer at any point.

Asking Questions

Throughout the process, you are an integral part of the dialogue. It is important to ask questions, not only to get answers but also to show interest. It is amazing to see applicants who never seek information, even when asked if they have any questions. An applicant who demonstrates no curiosity or the insight to ask questions probably will not make it to the next round. Also, the questions asked must be thoughtful and reflect the goals of the organization.

Some questions to ask include:

- What do you see as the biggest challenge of this job?
- What is your competitive advantage in this market?
- What are the best things about working here?
- How did you get to your position?
- What are the next steps in this process?

The ability to give and get information is critical. After all, you are going to make an important career and life decision. Table 3-3 shows an example of how a candidate might evaluate an opportunity prior to making a decision about interest in a position.

Moving Forward

As the interviews progress and you begin to see a viable role for you in the organization, seek feedback about the process and your performance from the hiring sponsor. He or she should be able and willing to tell you what is going well and what has gone poorly. You can then make corrections as needed.

If you are dropped from the process, by all means find out why. It may only be that the other candidates were stronger. But if it was due to a correctable issue, use the experience to learn.

If you come to the conclusion that you do not want the job, you have an obligation to handle the situation very professionally. You may want to communicate directly with the hiring manager and explain the reason you are withdrawing, or you may feel it more appropriate to work directly with the search firm executive. In either case, be professional, rational, and do not burn any bridges. There are a thousand scenarios of how to create a good ending. Be sure you work it through effectively.

Eventually, the offers will start coming in. You will have at least one, and probably several. They may be for different types of jobs, different challenges, and different situations. The good news is that your successful search has yielded enormous opportunities. The bad news is that you will have to choose from a plate of great opportunities. In this case, go back to your mentors/coaches. How can they help you talk through alternatives, get a financial analysis of the deal, and look at lifestyle issues. You are now ready to negotiate your future.

Table 3-3. Opportunity Evaluation

What I Want in a Job	Skills Needed	What the Job Offered
Responsibility	• Managerial/executive	• Management job in charge of two clinics and staffs • Supervision of a $100K outpatient business
Measurable and solid value	• Statistical measurement • Marketing/sales • Analytical thinking	• Need to increase profitability 20 percent in 18 months • Increase involvement by 15 percent in 1 year
Status and visibility	• Presentation skills • Executive presence	• One of the largest outpatient jobs in the state • Prestigious groups to work with
Creativity	• New approaches/ open mind	• Need high creativity to find new ways to improve quality and costs • New building project could be a challenge to design
Working with talented people, especially the boss	• Selection • Collegial • Team	• Superb boss by reputation • Select managers carefully—bright! • Can hire 2 managers
Chance to grow with the organization	• Increased knowledge of managed care • Network/negotiation skills	• Expected to grow to four clinics in three years • New network roles being designed
Learn new things	• Environmental scanning • Technology-based tools	• Experience in outpatient care and managed care • New physician relations to be built
Global experience	• Multicultural • International business	• Exploring service in Latin America • Can work with international team

Steps to a Health Care Career

Whether you stay in your current role, move to another, or create a new work world for yourself, there are several things you can do to constantly improve the health of your career. These include:

- Take stock periodically and plan now.
- Set both short- and long-term career goals.
- Focus on two or three goals each year to ensure new learning.
- Seek feedback.
- Keep up with the latest developments in your field.
- Learn to use the latest technology.
- Form relationships inside and outside your organization. Stay in touch with your network.
- Be visible. Join professional associations, speak, write, and volunteer for activities.
- Stay employable, flexible, and have a backup plan.
- Keep learning, increase your value, and market yourself.

Regardless of the path you choose to take, there will always be enormous opportunities in the field of health care. Make the most of your talent and your career. And by all means, never forget to help others.

Common Questions and Answers

Following are some common questions that people have about job loss. The answers provided encapsulate much of the information in this chapter.

- *How do I generate a network when I don't have one?* This is a fairly long-term issue. Although it is possible to develop a network in the short term, it is only possible if you devote enormous time and energy to it. The best way to develop a network is to work on it throughout your career. Take every opportunity to make contacts and have some semiregular conversations with people you think may be helpful to you later on or whom you might be able to help. For example, it is not uncommon to get phone calls from people who have just lost their jobs but who have made no prior effort to include you in their network. Interestingly, some of those people who ask for your assistance will not have either the courtesy to follow up or the interest to keep the relationship alive, even though you or they may need it some time in the future. Remember, networks are like plants — they require a lot of care in order to thrive.
- *Where do I go to find support during the search process?* Look in all the places where you normally find support — family, friends, church, professional colleagues, neighbors. People are willing to give support if they have some sort of an ongoing relationship but, again, the relationship has to be nurtured. There also is a point at which the people who are supporting you have to be able to say to you, "You're not doing enough with your search" or "I think you're depressed" or "You don't seem to be making much progress," and you have to be willing to listen to them. Having a support structure is absolutely critical during a job search.
- *Why didn't I make a decision earlier to make a career transition instead of waiting for some major change in the organization or getting to the point where I just could no longer go to work each day?* It is difficult to say why some people are not motivated to begin thinking pro-actively about their careers and making plans while they still have a job. For one thing, this is not always possible in today's chaotic world, where circumstances can change suddenly in organizations. You may not have any warning or the ability to do much in advance. Given the volatility of our present work world, people should take time to think about their careers and to ensure that they have the essential skill sets that will make them employable in a variety of settings.
- *Why won't prospective employers return my calls?* In the process of searching for a job, you will place hundreds of phone calls to

people. Some will be in an attempt to build a network, others will be in an attempt to actually find a hiring manager, and still others will be in response to an opportunity. Unfortunately, many calls will not be returned. Try not to take it personally. People are busy. If they do not know your name or whom you are connected with, they may make returning your call a low priority. To minimize this situation, the messages you leave on voice mail should be compelling and tied, if possible, to either someone you know in the organization or a recommendation you have had from one of his or her colleagues. You also can phone people more than once. You just have to be professional so that they do not consider you a pest. Whatever the case, one call may not be enough and you certainly must persevere.

- *Why is it taking so long to get a job?* It used to be a rule that for every $10,000 you make, it will take a month of searching to find a job. So the higher paid you were, the longer it would take. Whether this rule still holds true is questionable, but with the job market as tight and complex as it is today, a job search may take even longer. Often people who have been laid off or who have left a job want to take a breather and get their head together before they begin their job search. They may actually wait several months before beginning a search in earnest. Unfortunately, this leads to lost momentum and missed opportunities. Begin your search as soon and as aggressively as possible, and be persistent. The length of the search will be heavily influenced by the type of job you are looking for and the location.

- *When I go to interviews, how do I look energetic when I feel depressed?* First, if you know you are depressed, you should seek professional counseling. It is very, very difficult to interview and appear energetic when, in fact, you are being dragged down by your own mood swings. By and large, interviewers can see through that; and although you may say all the right things, if the interviewers do not see a level of energy, enthusiasm, or excitement, it is going to be very hard for them to support you as a candidate for their organization. Therefore, interview when you are at your best. If you are not having any success, ask the people in your peer group or your support group whether they think your mood is having a negative effect on your ability to project your best image.

- *What if I am applying for a job where I really don't have an exact experience match?* This is a common occurrence these days because of the growth of new segments in the health care industry. Consider, for example, managers and executives coming out of acute care settings who want to make the transition into alternative care delivery but lack experience in those areas. By breaking the job you are interested in into the component parts of finance, clinical management, quality improvement, and so on, and showing examples of how you have accomplished those things in your current position, you can demonstrate your qualifications. You also need to be able to link what you have done with the new opportunity. This requires a fair amount of thought about your experiences, not your jobs.

- *What should I do if I don't have computer skills or if I really can't use the Internet?* Computer skills are a distinct differentiator when you apply for a job, so it goes without saying that you need to be computer literate. Some organizations today simply will not hire you if you do not have basic computer skills. Beyond that, it is important to be able to use a computer to aid your job search.

- *Why is the Internet an important tool?* The speed and scope of the use of the Internet for job search is surprising. It is spreading quickly for both job hunting and hiring. In fact, the on-line network has turned into a bustling job bazaar where you can market your talents, find out what is happening, and perhaps even find the position you are looking for. The Internet is just simply too big to ignore, so it is important that you begin to think about shopping your services on-line. It is the ideal situation for those of you who may want to create nontraditional jobs, be a contract employee, or become a project manager. Consider reading *The On-Line Job Search Companion* by James Gonyea. It may prove a handy resource.

- *Exactly how does software read a resume?* Many companies, because they receive thousands of resumes a month, have turned to software programs that let them turn the resumes they receive into a database they can then search to fill job vacancies. For example, if they are looking for a nurse with 5 years of experience who also can speak Spanish and has ICU skills, the computer will provide a list of candidates who qualify. This makes it easier for the companies, but more difficult for the job seeker because you have to be able to describe your qualifications in a way the computer will recognize. For example, the misspelling of a critical word in a resume now can cause you to lose a job automatically because the computer will not pick up on a misspelled word. Also, you should not send your resume on any kind of colored paper or in color because color does not work well in scanners. Use a standard font and white paper. Do not dress up your resume with borders, boxes, or graphics, and keep the print on one side only. Computers can read very quickly, but they cannot turn over a sheet of paper.

- *What should my answering machine say?* This is a very important question because many people use their home answering machines to take messages and/or to screen calls. Clearly, this is not the time to have your children delivering a message or to have bells and whistles or the latest joke. If you are using your home answering machine as if it were your office, your message ought to reflect that. It should be professional, identify your name, and indicate that you will follow up immediately.

- *How can I be objective about accepting a job when I'm really hysterical?* It's easy for people to become hysterical when they have lost a job and are facing financial and professional challenges. One of the easiest things to do is to accept the first job that comes along. However, it may not be the right job. The easiest way to select the best job is to be absolutely sure you know what you want. So again, it goes back to clearly defining what you are after and working your plan in a reasonable way. The hardest thing you will ever do is to decline an offer because it is not exactly what you are looking for. However, to accept a job that is not what you are looking for will only mean that you will be back in the job market in a short period of time—and that is not good for either you or the employer.

- *What lessons have I learned from this search?* There are always lessons to be learned from life events, and a job search has its own set. One lesson you must hear quickly is to be disciplined in your search. On a more personal level, however, this is a time when you learn who your real friends and supporters are, and how you yourself can be a support system and a friend to others who are going through the same process. Last but not least, job searches often teach people that it is important to stay current, have contemporary skills, keep resumes up to date, and seek out experiences that will ensure lifelong employability. Perhaps the biggest lesson to be learned is that a job loss is not the end of the world. In fact, most people find opportunities that are better and pay more, and end up happier in the long run.

References

1. Bridges, W. *Job Shift.* New York City: Addison-Wesley, 1980.

2. Dent, H. *Job Shock.* New York City: St. Martin's Press, 1995.

3. Hyatt, C., and Gottlieb, L. *When Smart People Fail.* New York City: Penguin Books, 1993.

4. Hyatt and Gottlieb.

5. Gonyea, J. *The On-Line Job Search Companion.* New York City: McGraw-Hill, 1995.

Bibliography

Aley, T. The temp biz boom: why it's good. *Fortune* 132(8):53–55, Oct. 16, 1995.

Aley, T. What about you? *Fortune* 32(3):69–72, Aug. 7, 1995.

Bardsick, T. *Danger in the Comfort Zone.* New York City: AMACOM, 1991.

Bing, S. The seven habits of highly offensive people. *Fortune* 132(11):47–48, Nov. 27, 1995.

Boyett, T., and Conn, H. *Workplace 2000.* New York City: Dutton, 1991.

Bridges, W. *Job Shift.* New York City: Addison-Wesley, 1994.

Bridges, W. *Transitions.* New York City: Addison-Wesley, 1980.

Connelly, J. Have you gone as far as you can go? *Fortune* 130(13):231–32, Dec. 26, 1994.

Davidhizan, R. When you lose your job in healthcare management. *Healthcare Supervisor* 14(4):42–46, June 1996.

Dent, H. *Job Shock.* New York City: St. Martin's Press, 1995.

Farnham, A. Looking out for #1. *Fortune* 2(13):33–77, Jan. 15, 1994.

Gutteridge, T., Leibowitz, Z. B., and Shore, J. E. *Organizational Career Development.* San Francisco: Jossey-Bass, 1993.

Hyatt, C., and Gottlieb, L. *When Smart People Fail.* New York City: Penguin Books, 1993.

Kets De Vries, M. *Life and Death in the Executive Fast Lane.* San Francisco: Jossey-Bass, 1995.

Kravitz, D. *Getting Noticed.* New York City: John Wiley and Sons, 1985.

Larsen, E., and Goodstein, T. *Who's Driving Your Bus?* San Diego: Pfeiffer and Company, 1993.

Larson, T., and Comstock, C. *The New Rules of the Job Search Game.* Holbrook, MA: Bob Adams, 1994.

Noer, D. *Healing the Wounds.* San Francisco: Jossey-Bass, 1993.

Ryan, K., and Oestreich, D. *Driving Fear Out of the Workplace.* San Francisco: Jossey-Bass, 1991.

Saltzman, A. *Downshifting.* New York City: HarperCollins, 1991.

Scott, H., and Brudney, T. *Forced Out.* New York City: Fireside Books, 1987.

Sellers, P. So you failed: now bounce back. *Fortune* 131(8):48–66, May 1, 1995.

Stewart, T. The corporate jungle spawns a new species: the project manager. *Fortune* 132(1):179–180, July 10, 1995.

Swansburg, R., and Swansburg, P. *Strategic Career Planning and Development for Nurses.* Rockville, MD: Aspen, 1984.

Talley, M. *Career Hang Gliding.* New York City: Dutton, 1986.

Vestal, K. *Management Concepts for the New Nurse.* New York City: Lippincott, 1995.

Wexley, K., and Silverman, S. *Working Scanned.* San Francisco: Jossey-Bass, 1993.

Woodward, H., and Buchholz, S. *After Shock.* New York City: John Wiley and Sons, 1987.

Chapter 4

Achieving and Documenting Employment Agreements

JoAnne Kennebeck, JD, RN

Whether your employment status changes because of a change in your current organization or because you have elected to search for a new position in a new organization, you should give careful consideration to the matter of an employment contract. Although such contracts have long been standard practice in business and industrial firms, they have been less prevalent in the health care industry.[1] In the past 10 years, however, hospital CEOs in increasing numbers have entered into formal employment agreements. Currently, more than 40 percent of hospital CEOs have employment contracts and, according to the American Hospital Association, that number will grow.[2]

In turn, hospital CEOs have been more willing to extend this benefit to nurse executives. (Contracts for middle managers, however, are extremely rare; there is no reference to their existence in the literature.) In the past decade, nurse executive turnover has escalated and tenure has been decreasing.[3] With hospital executives expected to provide innovative leadership and control costs while maintaining quality of care, risk and vulnerability for all persons in key leadership roles have increased. Thus, an employment contract has become essential not only to describe and define job expectations, terms, and conditions of employment, but also to provide security in the event of changed circumstances.

This chapter discusses how to secure the terms and conditions of employment most important to you and how to reduce the agreements you make with your employer to a legally enforceable form. Because each executive's personal situation and priorities are different, and each employment setting offers different opportunities and challenges, the terms and conditions of every employement arrangement must be set accordingly. Further, if these concerns are addressed in the employment negotiations but not converted to a legally enforceable instrument, they may be invalid. This chapter helps you avoid the potentially disastrous consequences of undocumented employment agreements.

Making the Case for a Contract

Historically, employers and boards have disliked the idea of employment agreements with executives, because contracts, to some degree, limit their authority and freedom. Some feel that the request to "put it in writing" indicates a lack of trust. However, a contract is primarily a matter of equitably balancing rights, privileges, and protections for both employer and employee. Fortunately, more and more boards and corporate executives are viewing the employment contract as a means of attracting and retaining the best talent, as well as encouraging and supporting innovative leadership. Further, a well-structured contract can provide a means by which disagreements in the professional relationship can be resolved amicably. A carefully considered and well-drafted employment contract offers definite advantages to both parties to the agreement.

Introducing the Idea of a Contract

Accepting a position in a new organization has been the most common method of making a career change. It also presents one of the easiest occasions to introduce the idea of an employment contract. Different approaches may be considered, but the subject typically is not raised until the interviews are complete, you have been offered the job, and you have decided you want it. You may then raise the issue as a matter of course. This is easiest if:

- You know the employer has used employment contracts with other executives.
- You had a contract in a previous job.
- Contracts are a routine practice in the industry.[4]

If the job is especially risky or the organizational environment particularly chaotic, you may raise the matter with an observation of those facts, expressing the concern that, even if you perform exceedingly well in the CEO's view, other forces may put your job on the line. You query as to how your interests may be protected.

In this way, you have introduced the idea of a contract without making it "the issue." This gives the employer the opportunity to continue discussing the matter of a contract if he or she is concerned about it. You may respond by saying that you assumed the organization would want a written agreement. Of course, you may decide the direct approach is better for your situation and raise the issue straight out in the course of negotiations. For example, you might say: "It has been my experience that reducing an employment agreement to writing helps avoid future conflicts and frees me to turn my full attention to the work at hand. Would you mind putting this agreement in writing?"

On the other hand, if you have never had an employment contract before, you might acknowledge that, but then explain that the job you have been offered involves considerable challenge and substantial commitment on your part. You want to make it clear that you are eager to begin but would appreciate the security that a written agreement provides.

Supporting Your Request for a Contract

Because an employment contract has become more common for health care executives/administrators, the idea may not be as unnerving to the employer as it once was, particularly if he or she has such an agreement. On the other hand, it could become an issue because it is less common for nurse executives/managers to have or seek employment contracts. Concerns about authority, control, and trust may trouble the employer. You can address these concerns by saying that you believe a contract:

- Is a useful way of documenting mutual agreement
- Provides a means of clarifying points discussed
- Prevents future misunderstandings

In essence, a contract leaves both parties free to focus on the organizational work to be done.

If the concern is one of trust or commitment, you may point out that you would not engage in employment discussions at all unless you were willing to commit yourself completely to the job and the organization. Or you might say that you would not consider working for or with a person or organization you did not trust. The contract merely documents the details of the employment arrangement and is a resource if future questions arise.

The situation may call for a more candid response if you are being asked to undertake a very pivotal role in an organization undergoing rapid and dramatic change. You know you will be required to make unpopular and highly politicized decisions that will make you a target for unhappy physicians and staff. It may be best to confront that circumstance head on. The matter has little to do with trusting that your employer will support you through crisis. Experienced executives know that in this complex and chaotic environment, forces beyond the control of any single person may dictate unexpected outcomes. Executives and managers, through no fault of their own, may become victims of these forces. Although a contract cannot prevent this from happening, it can protect your job or at least your income in the event that unexpected circumstances arise. It lessens the likelihood that you will be terminated on some arbitrary point and secures your personal circumstances if you find yourself suddenly unemployed. A contract also may assist the employer in defending your continued employment in the face of serious external pressures. A frank discussion of these points with your prospective employer, if this is your situation, may make the sensibility of a written employment agreement obvious to all.

When you accept a new position, it is important in these troubled times to be sure that the terms and conditions of employment are very clear. The best way to achieve this is to document them in writing. Documentation of work done and agreements reached is second nature to the professional nurse in her or his clinical practice. In this most important matter, the job itself, that same attention to documentation is vital.

If the employer resists, keep pressing as diplomatically as possible, suggesting at the least use of a memorandum or letter of agreement. Even acknowledgment by the employer that putting a few points in writing (even if it is not a formal contract) will be acceptable provides reasonable assurance that you will end up with some form of written agreement.

Dealing with an Employer's Refusal to Consider a Contract

What if the employer flatly refuses to consider a written agreement? In this event, you must decide whether you can get enough in compensation and perks to make up for the lack of a contract or else withdraw from negotiations. Although withdrawal may seem extreme, it must be considered in light of the professional and personal risks you are being asked to assume.[5] If the risks are serious and considerable, the employer's refusal to limit your exposure may be a harbinger of the future. If they are not, or if you are being compensated sufficiently to assume them, you may choose to accept the position without a written contract.

Navigating the Negotiation Process

R. Fisher and W. Ury define *negotiation* as a basic means of getting what you want from others.[6] They describe it as a back-and-forth communication designed to reach agreement when you and the other side have some interests that are shared and others that are opposed.

There are no hard-and-fast rules about negotiation. As much depends on the circumstances as on the parties participating. The circumstances bringing you and your employer to the table will have a tremendous effect on the tone and nature of the discussions.

The Prenegotiation Phase

In the prenegotiation stage, you will need to accomplish two things. First, you will need to identify and prioritize your and your prospective employer's interests; and, second, you will need to research the market.

Identify and Prioritize Both Parties' Interests

If this is a new employment situation and the prospective employer is accustomed to employment contracts, and if your intentions as to the terms and conditions are clarified, the negotiations may feel more relaxed. However, if the situation is one of a merger, acquisition, or restructuring, the uncertainties or anxieties about new relationships with old competitors may create additional stress and mistrust for both parties.

Identifying Your Prospective Employer's Interests
Whatever the situation, it is important to understand your prospective employer's interests, both professional and personal. What are the organization's objectives in this negotiation, and thus your prospective employer's objectives in securing your employment? What limitations have been placed on your prospective employer? Will other employment contracts be modeled after this one, making it precedent setting? Are you going to request terms or conditions that exceed current organizational policy or pay practices? The employer's agenda will cover priorities such as controlling costs, getting and keeping the best available talent, and locking you into the organization on terms that are advantageous to the employer and also make you happy.

The employer's personal agenda has more to do with his or her own personality and experience with contract negotiations. It tends to be influenced by his or her general approach to problem solving, whether from an analytical, conceptual, organizational, or interpersonal perspective.[7] It is advantageous to learn as much as possible about the prospective employer prior to the negotiation process in order to better understand the person and his or her management style. This will enable you to design your approach to address the employer's agenda. Considering the other party's interests prior to entering into actual negotiations will help prepare you. Taking time to thoroughly assess the other party's interests, write them down, and prioritize them as your knowledge of the person permits will serve you well during the course of your discussions. This will alert you to opportunities to serve the other party's interests, making it easier for him or her to serve yours[8] and, ultimately, for you both to reach agreement. For example, your prospective employer may have experienced unacceptable levels of turnover in the position being offered to you, so he or she may view stability, or at least an assurance of some sort of semipermanence, as a priority. Your ability and willingness to forego other opportunities and make an extended commitment may well address the employer's interest. Once the employer's interest is satisfied, you can more readily open discussion of your concerns.

At its heart, negotiation is an adversarial process. The parties coming together have different interests and different agendas. Optimally, negotiation will lead to an agreement that serves the interests of both parties, but it is imperative that you understand the true nature of the process. The temptation to be a "nice guy" or to "go easy" because you do not want to jeopardize your future relationship with your boss is misguided. Not only will you fail to have your interests met in the ensuing agreement, you may feel resentful toward your new employer and angry with yourself for "giving in or up." Both will impair your ability to get off to a good start in your new position. A professional relationship is not damaged by tough negotiation.[9]

Identifying Your Interests

Critical to protecting your interests is understanding clearly what they are. Fisher and Ury define *interests* as needs, desires, concerns, or fears.[10] They are motivators, and cause us to take a position on a certain issue. Your interests in an employment agreement may be salary, job security following a merger, or a severance package that protects you if your position is eliminated during a future restructuring or downsizing. You may be concerned that you could become a target for unhappy physicians or disgruntled staff if you fulfill the responsibilities of your new role, and may want the criteria for evaluating your performance to be very specific and relevant.

You must spend the time necessary to clearly identify and prioritize your interests as related to this specific employment situation. Once you have done this, it is very useful to write them down in descending order. They can and should become a constant resource throughout the negotiation process.

Research the Market

Once you have identified and prioritized both parties' interests, you will need additional information about the market before you begin negotiations. A literature search of periodicals published by professional human resource associations is a good resource for information on current salary and benefit packages. It is important to learn as much as you can about different compensation and severance options because there may be several different methods to protect your interest in job security or an income stream if your position is eliminated. Having considered multiple ways to address your needs gives you an advantage in the negotiating process. You will appear reasonable and flexible. You will be able to offer your employer choices and the opportunity to feel "in charge" of the process without compromising your own interests. For example, you suggest deferred income options in lieu of present income. You may request a company car, paid membership in professional organizations, or other options in place of a higher salary.

One of the most useful guides to principled negotiations can be found in *Getting to Yes: Negotiating Agreement without Giving In*[11] and the companion book, *Getting Together: Building Relationships As We Negotiate.*[12] Principled negotiations are those that decide issues on their merits rather than through a process focused on what each side says it will and will not do. Fisher and Ury suggest that you look for mutual gains wherever possible and that where interests conflict, the result be based on some fair standard, independent of the will of either side.[13] For example, in negotiating a compensation package, you might select the Hay Hospital Compensation Survey as a guide.[14] You might agree to accept an average for your position in hospitals your size in your region of the country. Other organizations, associations, and consulting firms also have compensation data, and you and your employer might select one of them as an objective outside standard.

Both books mentioned above focus on substantive and specific means to achieve a mutually beneficial agreement while maintaining or enhancing the relationship between the parties. This is particularly important where employment agreements are concerned. You may get the salary terms and conditions you desire if they want you badly enough, but if the relationship with your prospective employer is damaged in the process, your success with the organization may be at risk. On the other hand, if the appearance of a friendly relationship is preserved at the expense of your interests, the resulting agreement will do little to support your success and satisfaction in your new role.

The basic precepts of Ury, Fisher, and S. Brown's books are as follows:[15,16]

1. *Separate the emotional or relationship issues from the substantive ones.* For example, you feel frustrated and angry because you feel the employer is trying to secure your services for the lowest possible price when, in fact, he or she is trying to stay within the paid salary guidelines applied to other similar positions in the organization. Other forms of compensation may be an option and serve both parties' interests. Fair and acceptable compensation is the substantive issue.

2. *Focus on interests, not positions.* For example, stating that your salary must be *x* dollars is a position and a decision when your interests

in an equitable compensation package may be served by alternatives to salary alone.

3. *Invent options for mutual gain.* For example, you suggest alternatives to salary, such as deferred income, memberships, tuition, or other options that allow the employer to stay within his or her constraints while meeting your needs.

4. *Use objective criteria that are legitimate and practical.* For example, you may suggest using data from recognized associations or organizations as a guideline for acceptability of a compensation package.

This approach permits both parties to focus together on the problems before them rather than on each other's role or position relative to the problem. For example, the issue may be providing for retirement. Your interest is less in current income than it is in contributing to your retirement fund. The company, on the other hand, is not interested in creating a separate retirement plan for you at a higher rate than your peers in the company. If you hold fast to the percentage contribution you believe you need, you place the negotiator in a win-or-lose situation. However, if you clearly articulate your interest, which is funding your retirement, you may devise ways to defer current income without disturbing the general benefit plan. In this way, both parties achieve their goals and neither feels compromised.

The Different Contract Forms

All employment relationships are based on some type of agreement. If you do *x* for me, I will do *y* for you. The agreement may be oral or written, and may or may not be enforceable by law. The written agreement may take one of the following forms:

- An offer letter and acceptance
- A letter of agreement
- A comprehensive written formal contract

Every enforceable contract has three essential elements: the offer, consideration, and acceptance. In this situation, the *offer*, made either orally or in writing, comes in the form of the employer offering the prospective employee work. K. H. Decker and H. T. Felix describe the offer as follows:

The offer must contain the contract's essential terms and conditions. To form the contract, the offeror and offeree must agree to the same terms and conditions at the same time; that is, mutual assent or a meeting of the minds must result from the same understanding of what the offer is. No contract arises unless the employee and the employer agree to the same employment terms and conditions at the same time. It is what the employee and employer do, not what each thinks, that controls in creating the employment relationship.[17]

Consideration is the thing of value that is promised or given. In the employment setting, consideration may be the employee's promise to work in exchange for the employer's promise to pay a certain salary, benefit, and so on.

The final element is *acceptance*. To create a binding employment contract, the employee must accept the offer voluntarily and unequivocally. No written agreement is necessary, but without it, the terms and conditions offered and accepted may be unclear or misunderstood.

Offer Letter and Acceptance

In this form of contract, the employer sends or delivers a letter to the prospective employee offering him or her a specific position. Generally, included in the letter is a description of the duties, compensation, benefits, and any other essential term or condition of employment given in return for work to be performed. The letter also should name a date after which the offer will be withdrawn. The offer letter may be sent on its own, or it may document an earlier discussion between the prospective employer and employee. Once the prospective employee receives the letter, he or she may accept or reject the offer either orally or in writing. Failure to respond within the time frame stated in the letter may constitute a rejection.

If you receive an offer letter in which all the terms and conditions desired by you are not documented, you may reply with a counteroffer. A counteroffer, instead of an acceptance or refusal of the offer of employment, sets forth new or additional terms to the original offer for the employer to accept or reject. Again, the essential elements of an offer, consideration, and acceptance must be present before an agreement is legally binding. Once the offer has been accepted, the accepting party should document the acceptance in the form of a letter of response.

An offer letter and corresponding letter of acceptance are the simplest and most common form of documenting an employment agreement. They provide some protection to the parties in that the essential, if not all, the terms and conditions of employment are listed in writing. Later misunderstandings due to failed memory or misinterpretation are less likely with an offer letter and letter of acceptance. Such a letter is advantageous in a situation where the employer may be unwilling to document a more formal or complete agreement. Its main disadvantage is that many other issues of employment may not be included and cannot be inferred later if questions arise. Sample letters documenting an offer and an acceptance are shown in figures 4-1 and 4-2, respectively.

Letter of Agreement

A letter of agreement is used frequently and seems to serve quite satisfactorily despite the fact that it does not cover many contingencies. It is simply a letter from employer to employee documenting the terms already agreed to in an earlier discussion between them. As the recipient of a letter of agreement, it is essential that you check carefully to make sure all agreed-to terms are included. If they are not, you must respond, preferrably in writing, and request the necessary additions. You also must make clear that your acceptance of the offer is conditional upon the employer's written response.

Generally, a letter of agreement can be used in situations where it is thought difficult or inappropriate to negotiate on all the incidental terms that would be included in a more formal contract. However, it does provide some assurance of continued employment at some reasonable salary. It also may address one or two of the most important employment matters, such as noncompete clauses, severance pay, or specific concerns in a benefit package.[18]

If the employee does not have a formal contract, a letter of agreement also may be very useful to document the terms of a severance package offered and accepted when an employee's position has been eliminated or realigned during a restructuring, merger, or other major organizational change. Again, the main disadvantage is that other important issues of employment are not addressed and cannot be inferred later if questions arise.

Sample letters of agreement are provided in figures 4-3 and 4-4. Although sample letter 4-3 sounds less formal than 4-4, it is binding nevertheless.

Formal Employment Contract

A formal employment contract sets forth in writing all the terms and conditions of an employment relationship and is signed by both parties to the agreement. Usually, the parties to the agreement enlist the assistance of legal counsel in drafting and reviewing the document, because the legal intricacies of the formal contract may well be beyond their expertise. They may unwittingly negate or render unenforceable parts or all of the contract by using terms or incorporating clauses that are too broad or have legal meanings beyond the parties' intentions. Separate legal counsel for each party can protect the individuals' interests as well as ensure overall enforceability of the contract.

Figure 4-1. Sample Offer Letter

ABC MEDICAL ASSOCIATES
A Preferred Provider Organization

December 6, 1994

JoAnne Jones
#1 Happy Street
Merryville, IA 50021

Dear JoAnne:

We certainly enjoyed the opportunity to visit with you and discuss employment opportunities at ABC Associates, Inc. Barb and I were favorably impressed with your qualifications.

I would like to offer you the position of Utilization Management Coordinator. This is a new position within our organization and would function in the manner we discussed. I anticipate that further clarification of the role will be done once the position is filled. Because the position is new, the individual filling it will have a great deal of input and latitude in the shaping of the scope of job responsibilities.

I am prepared to make you the following offer:

Salary:	$13.47 per hour (This would equal $14,000/year at an average of 20 hrs/wk.)
Health insurance:	Single coverage paid by ABC Medical Associates; eligible after 30 days of employment
Dental coverage:	Single coverage paid by ABC following six months of employment
Vacation:	Accrued at the rate of .038 of an hour for each hour worked
Sick leave:	Accrued at the rate of .038 of an hour for each hour worked
Life insurance:	Term life insurance one times the annual salary can be purchased by the employee at the group rates obtained by ABC.

Start date: January 7, 1995

(Continued on next page)

Figure 4-1.   (Continued)

Page 2

Obviously, we are flexible on the start date. Should you want to move the date one way or the other, I would be more than willing to make an appropriate change.

Should you have any questions or want to discuss any of these items, please feel free to give me a call.

I am looking forward to your reply on or before December 15.

Sincerely,

James A. Smith
President

Figure 4-2. Sample Letter of Acceptance

December 10, 1994

James A. Smith
President
ABC Medical Associates

Dear Mr. Smith:

I am in receipt of your letter dated December 6, 1994, offering me the position of Utilization Management Coordinator. I am challenged and excited by the prospect of joining ABC Medical Associates and developing this new position which I understand to be designing and implementing a utilization review and management system. The salary and benefit program outlined in your letter are consistent with the terms we discussed during my interview.

I am pleased to accept your offer and will report to the offices of ABC Medical Associates on January 7, 1995, at 7 a.m. I look forward to working with you and Mrs. Barbara White. Thank you for this opportunity.

Sincerely,

JoAnne Smith

Figure 4-3.   Sample Letter of Agreement (Informal)

MEMORIAL HOSPITAL
Medical Center

November 5, 1995

Mr. John Doe
1120 James Street
Baja, CA 77788

Dear John,

This letter will outline our understanding and your acceptance of the position of Senior Vice President here at Memorial Hospital Medical Center. Your official arrival date will be December 9, 1995. This will give you time to finalize various issues in Baja.

I'm extremely delighted and excited about your acceptance of our offer of this position. I feel, as do all of the management staff, that you will be an asset to this facility and our management team. We are also excited about the prospect of your joining us for what I hope becomes a mutually beneficial relationship for MHMC and you.

We have some incredible opportunities and challenges facing us throughout our industry and in Jessup. However, we anticipate having some fun as we work hard to accomplish goals that are good for this organization as well as provide significant opportunities for personal and professional development.

Welcome aboard!

Let me summarize my understanding of our verbal agreement Friday, regarding the elements of your employment with us:

1.   The salary will be $110,000 annually, effective December 1, 1995. Because you will be paid on a monthly basis, you will receive your first paycheck in January. Beginning with FY 1996, you will be paid on a per pay period basis. In March 1997, you will be eligible for any appropriate salary increase under our Pay for Performance program. We currently do not have a senior-level management incentive program, but I anticipate reinstating such for the 1996 calendar year.

Figure 4-3. (Continued)

Page 2

2. We will provide reimbursement for all closing costs relating to the sale of your house in Baja. We will also cover full relocation expenses, including: personal food, lodging, and auto for your relocation travel to Jessup. We have a corporate relocation/moving program with Bekins Van Lines, and Joanne can provide you with all the necessary details.
3. I understand and support the need for several "house hunting" trips back and forth between Baja and Jessup.
4. A monthly car allowance of $350.00 will be provided.
5. A monthly housing allowance of $500.00 will be provided for up to six (6) months or until you find a permanent residence, whichever is the shorter period of time.
6. Our severance policy for executives will include a period of up to nine (9) months and outplacement support of up to $15,000.

Benefits

A. *Pension plan:* The Medical Center has in place a defined contribution, contributory pension plan that requires a two-year eligibility waiting period; however, the program is fully vested after this two-year waiting period. This plan does require some employee matching contribution through available TSA products. More information is available in the Personnel Department.
B. *Health/dental:* The Medical Center's basic plan for all employees who work over 24 hours per week is through First Choice Health Plan, Inc. The Medical Center pays for your premium and through a "gross-up" arrangement provides monies for dependent coverage. In addition, we have an HMO alternative—HealthPlus. In the event you select the HMO option, the Medical Center will pay the same as described above for First Choice. Your coverage will go into effect March 1, 1996.
C. *Life insurance:* The Medical Center's basic life insurance plan, which pays the premium for all employees who work over 24 hours per week, is equal to two and one-half times annual salary. There are opportunities to purchase additional group term life insurance as well as dependent term life insurance.
D. *Disability insurance:* Following a 90-day waiting period, the Medical Center pays the premium for an excellent long-term disability program.
E. *Vacation:* You will accrue vacation at the rate of four (4) weeks per year, beginning immediately upon employment. You are eligible to take accrued hours after six (6) months of employment.

(Continued on next page)

Figure 4-3.   (Continued)

Page 3

F. *Sick leave:* The Medical Center has a fairly typical sick leave policy which
    is available to all employees and accrues at one day per month, up to a
    maximum of 90 days (720 hours).
G. *Holidays:* We have nine (9) holidays per year—New Year's, President's Day,
    Memorial Day, Fourth of July, Labor Day, Thanksgiving, Christmas,
    birthday, and personal day.

John, I believe this covers the areas of our understanding and the major
benefit areas. You can get more detailed information from Joanne.

Please confirm your acceptance of this offer and agreement to me in writing
by November 15, 1995.

There's a lot of work to be done, and we're glad that you are going to be
joining us to help us serve this community.

Again, our sincere welcome to you and Linda as you join Memorial Hospital
Medical Center and the Jessup community.

Sincerely,

Michael J. Lake
President & CEO

cc: Joanne Blume, Vice President Human Resources

Source: Yancer, D. *Career Connections.* Seattle: American Organization of Nurse Executives, 1995.

Figure 4-4. Sample Letter of Agreement (Formal)

_____
(Date)

Dear _____:

_____ Hospital desires to secure your services for
a period of _____ years as Chief Nursing Executive of the Hospital
Corporation, the duties of which are stated in the job description attached to
this letter. As Chief Nursing Executive, you will report directly to the Chief
Executive Officer.

For your services as Chief Nursing Executive, the Hospital agrees to pay you a
salary of $_____ per annum or such higher figure as shall be agreed
upon at an annual review of your compensation. This annual review shall occur
prior to the end of each year of this agreement for the express purpose of
considering increments. The amount of $_____ shall be payable in
equal monthly installments throughout the contract year. You may, at your
option, require that such portion of this said salary as you may designate be
put into tax-sheltered investments and treated as deferred income.

This agreement is not intended to, and in fact does not, incorporate any
benefits of your employment other than those stated in this letter. All other
benefits of your employment, as determined at the time of the annual review,
will be negotiated separately from, and will not be included as part of, this
agreement.

(Insert list of agreed-upon fringe benefits here.)

It is understood that the Hospital may, in its discretion, terminate your duties
as Chief Nursing Executive. Upon termination, all rights, duties, and obligations
of both parties shall cease, except that the Hospital shall continue to pay you
your then monthly salary for the month in which your duties were terminated
and for twenty-four consecutive months thereafter as an agreed-upon
termination payment. During this period, you shall not be required to come to
the Hospital or to perform any duties for the Hospital, nor shall the fact that
you seek, accept, and undertake other employment during this period affect
such payments. Also, during this period, the Hospital agrees to keep your
group life insurance and health insurance benefits, as enumerated above, fully
paid up and in effect.

Should the Hospital, at its discretion, change your duties so it can reasonably
be found that you are no longer performing the duties of the Chief Nursing
Executive of the Hospital, you shall have the right, in your complete discretion,

---

(Continued on next page)

Figure 4-4.   (Continued)

Page 2

to terminate this agreement by written notice delivered to the Chief Executive
Officer. Upon such termination, all rights, duties, and obligations of both
parties shall cease, except that the Hospital shall continue to pay you your
then monthly salary for the month in which your duties were terminated and
for twenty-four consecutive months thereafter as the agreed-upon termination
payment. During this period you shall not be required to come to the Hospital
or to perform any duties for the Hospital, nor shall the fact that you seek,
accept, or undertake other employment during this term affect such payments.
Also, during this period, the Hospital agrees to keep your group life insurance
and health insurance benefits, as enumerated above, fully paid up and in
effect.

By mutual agreement of the parties, this agreement and all of its terms and
conditions may be extended from year to year, or for a term beyond its initial
term, by a letter to that effect exchanged between the parties at any time
during the agreement period.

(Name of Hospital)

BY: _____
        (Chief Executive Officer)

I accept the offer contained in
the above letter.

_____

Date: _____

Source: American College of Hospital Administrators. Contracts for hospital chief executive officers.
In: *Report of the Ad Hoc Committee on Contracts for Hospital Chief Executive Officers.* Chicago:
ACHA, 1982, p. 57.

Advantages of a Written Contract

One advantage of a comprehensive written document is that little about the employment relationship is left to later interpretation or misinterpretation, depending on your point of view. The employee's position is protected in the event of a changing administration and from the vagaries of the highly politicized modern hospital environment. The employee can proceed to the difficult or risky aspects of the work she or he was employed to do while being assured that she or he will not become the scapegoat if physicians, peers, or subordinates become unhappy with the direction taken. The employer also has the advantage of using the contract to forestall detractors and prevent premature or ill-conceived action on the employer's part. Thus a comprehensive contract may benefit both employee and employer.

A well-written contract will contain a general list of duties as well as any specific expectations. Expectations may take the form of special projects such as merging the nursing divisions of two merging hospitals or computerizing the documentation system. This kind of specificity is helpful to employer and employee alike when prioritizing performance goals and evaluating same.

Other advantages include:

- Specification of the employee's and employer's responsibilities and obligations
- Setting of the contract's duration, after which all employee and employer obligations automatically cease without the liability arising out of normal employment terminations
- Identification of the remedies available for the contract's breach
- Provision for a dispute resolution mechanism to settle problems that arise under the contract without resort to costly and time-consuming court litigation[19]

Disadvantages of a Written Contract

The primary disadvantage of a formal contract is that both parties are bound by the words it contains. This means that it lacks the flexibility of a less formal arrangement. It may seem that all possible contingencies have been provided for and, in fact, all forseeable problems may have been addressed at the time of the writing. However, today's complex and changing health care environment holds surprises for even the most seasoned administrator. A comprehensive contract may make it more difficult to adapt quickly and easily to changing circumstances. That is not to say that the contract cannot be changed or modified by mutual consent; it can. However, to make a change, you will likely need to consult with attorneys, which can be time consuming and expensive.

Problems also may arise in the interpretation and administration of the contract. It is very important that the terms of the contract be clear and unambiguous. Legalisms such as *whosoever, whensoever, wheresoever, whatsoever, aforesaid, hereinafter, thereunto,* and so on should be avoided. Words not used in daily conversation and which do not add to the clear meaning of the document should not be used.

The Elements of a Contract

You will want to ensure that your contract agreement covers a number of basic elements. Following are descriptions of those elements most often deemed important to executive employees.

General Statement of Employment

Every contract should contain a general statement acknowledging that the nurse executive and the institution intend to create an employment relationship based on the terms and conditions set forth in the agreement. This general paragraph defines the rights and responsibilities of the parties and specifically references the other provisions of the agreement.[20] This paragraph also clearly and specifically identifies the parties to the agreement. This is very important because it limits legal standing of those who may challenge the agreement later.

Position Description

The employment agreement should contain a provision that describes the duties of the nurse executive. Generally, the nurse executive is obliged to perform those specified duties within the policies, rules, and procedures of the hospital or health care facility. From the employer's perspective, it is important to have the nurse executive agree to faithfully serve the institution and to devote the time necessary for the adequate performance of duties. From the nurse executive's perspective, this provision should clearly specify what is expected of her. A general job description in addition to the reporting responsibilities should be included. From the nurse executive's perspective, a good provision to include is one allowing him or her to have a direct reporting relationship to top management.[21]

Specific projects and expectations should be listed separately in this general section, especially if they will provide a significant basis for the performance appraisal or if they infer risks that may politicize the evaluation of the nurse executive's performance. For example, if you are expected to restructure a part of the organization, which implies a work force reduction, it may be wise to have that documented.

Performance Goals and Evaluation Mechanisms

Evaluation criteria and time frames are important to include, especially if special performance goals are part of the agreement. For example, if a restructuring with work force reduction is part of the agreement, you may want to include the numbers that will define the project as being successful for the employer. Criteria should be specific, outcome oriented, measurable, and achievable. The achievability factor is critical. Goals that are too broad or that rely on the support of persons you do not control should not be included. You do not want the opinions of an influential, but occasionally hostile player (such as the chief of the medical staff) determining how well you are doing your job.

It also may be useful to document how the process of goal setting will be achieved. For example, in the work force example, are you expected to achieve the targets through attrition, layoffs, a combination of both, or some other method entirely? You may want to ensure in writing that it requires mutual assent. Goals set unilaterally by the employer may be unachievable, thus positioning you for termination for failure to perform.

The schedule or timing of the performance evaluation also is important to include. It may be appropriate to start with 6-month intervals and annually thereafter. You may wish to include terms that provide the opportunity for self-evaluations or the opportunity to respond to the employer evaluation included.

Compensation and Periodic Review Schedule

Salary may be considered the most important provision of the contract by the employee. Certainly, it is key. Wages or salary usually will be described in an annual amount, followed by payment frequency and a date when payments will start. Salary ranges will vary, based on the responsibilities and scope of the job, whether it is in the public or private sector, and where it is located geographically.

It is important that you do your homework before addressing the issue of salary. You need to find out what others in like positions in your region of the country are making. The Hay Hospital Compensation Survey is an excellent reference.[22] Colleagues in similar positions may help you identify an acceptable range for a particular position, even if they are unwilling to share personal information. Careful review of the job directories in professional journals also can be helpful in establishing a range for a given position in a specific part of the country.

If accepting this position requires a move to another part of the country, it is very important to find out the cost-of-living differences from your present location. What may seem like a substantial increase on its face actually may be a reduction when housing and other costs are taken into consideration. Information on the cost-of-living differences can be obtained from U.S. Commerce Department Statistical Abstracts found at your local public library. Another useful source is *Places Rated,* which is available at most bookstores.[23]

Bonuses or Other Pay-for-Performance Concepts
Bonuses or other pay-for-performance concepts, often used by businesses, may be another way for the nurse executive to reach her or his compensation goals. Usually, these compensation options are tied to the financial performance of either the organization as a whole or the executive division alone.

You should not include the possibility of bonuses or other pay concepts tied to future events in evaluating the sufficiency of the salary for the responsibilities of the job. Most important, you should be satisfied that the compensation package equals the responsibilities and risks of the job.

Incentive Stock Options and Profit-Sharing Plans
With the growth of investor-owned hospitals and health care systems, alternative compensation options have become available to health care executives. Profit-sharing plans and incentive stock options are two such alternatives.

A *stock option* is the right given by companies to key employees to buy some of the company's shares at a favorable price. Stock options are an incentive to attract and retain key employees.[24] As J. Tarrant explains in *Perks and Parachutes*:

> The Tax Reform Act of 1981 has made this device attractive to employees by reducing the tax rate on capital gains; by decreeing that no taxes need be paid until the stock has actually been sold; and by assuring capital-gains treatment if the shares are held for one year after they are bought. The recipient of the option must wait two years before exercising the option. The option cannot be exercised more than three months after the recipient ceases active employment with the company. If these provisions are not met, the profit is taxable as ordinary income.[25]

Profit sharing plans are essentially bonus plans based on a distribution of a percentage of an organization's net profits. A variation on profit sharing can be a contribution by the employer to a 401(k) or 403(b) plan above and beyond the usual employer contribution. The advantage to the employee is the tax-deferred status of these contributions.[26]

Some organizations may offer their executive employees the opportunity to participate in other deferred compensation plans. Always inquire about this option.

Compensation Review

It is a good idea to include a plan for compensation review in the contract. A clause that allows automatic increases over a period of years would be preferable but may not be agreeable to the employer. In lieu of automatic increases, a clause that requires a review of the executive's salary at regular intervals is important. It provides the opening for the discussion that otherwise might be difficult for the employee to request. A 6-month initial review with annual reviews thereafter is common. However, setting a specific date ensures that the review will occur.

Benefits

Other benefits that may be included in the total compensation package and which thus should be included in the contract are vacation time, sick leave, medical disability and life insurance, company car, dues for professional associations and service organizations, reimbursement for job-related expenses, and a retirement plan. This list is not intended to be inclusive.

Vacation Time

Generally, vacation and holiday pay is considered part of a compensation package and should be addressed specifically in the contract.[27] Employees want a vacation clause specifying that they can use their accrued vacation without having to meet length-of-service requirements as a condition. However, employers would prefer language that requires actual service on a specified date for vacation pay to accrue.[28] When drafting the vacation clause, consider accrual rate, eligibility and use requirements, consequences of failure to use, and carryover and payout on termination or retirement.[29]

Sick Leave

If sick leave is not included in the contract, there will be no obligation to pay on the part of the employer. Terms to be included in the sick leave clause include accrual and payment rate, carryover year to year, and payout at termination or retirement.[30]

Some organizations have adopted policies that combine vacation, holiday, and sick time benefits into a paid time off (PTO) package in lieu of handling them separately. The same contract issues apply. Include accrual rate, eligibility and use requirements, carryover, payout, and so on.

Medical Disability and Life Insurance

Medical disability and life insurance also should be included in this section of the contract. Usually, the medical plan will be the same as that offered to other employees, but the nurse executive can negotiate additional coverage in the form of payment of deductibles or coinsurance. In addition to basic and major medical benefits, coverage for dental and eye care could be included. Family or dependent coverage also should be addressed at this time. Premium payment can be covered by the employer or shared by the employee, so these terms must be negotiated and included in the contract.[31]

Disability plans vary widely, so it is important to include specific terms that may be important to you. Basic considerations include benefit type (short and/or long term), payment, eligibility, and coordination with other benefits such as sick leave and unpaid leave.[32]

Life insurance also should be included in this section of the contract. In addition to dollar amounts, which should be a minimum of two to three times the executive's annual salary, coverage for family members could be included.

Company Car

Some organizations may be induced to provide a company car or automobile allowance to the executive, especially if he or she has responsibilities at more than one site or campus. With increasing numbers of mergers, acquisitions, and joint operating ventures, more and more executives will be expected to work at several different locations, often in the same day. Terms to consider including are availability and usage, along with replacement time frames.

Dues for Professional Associations and Service Organizations

If you want to ensure that dues for professional associations and service organizations are included, a clause stating same should be included in the contract. If you are expected to belong to any private clubs in order to socialize with other executives of your rank or members of the medical staff and so on, negotiate inclusion of those dues in the agreement. It may be helpful to list the associations, organizations, and clubs specifically. If the job requires special licenses, certifications, or registrations, the cost of retaining these designations could be negotiated and included in this clause.

Reimbursement for Job-Related Expenses

It is customary to reimburse employees for job-related expenses. Clauses usually cover expense reporting, travel and entertainment, or business travel expenses. Although most clauses focus on reimbursable expenses and expense-reporting procedures for travel outside the area where the employer is located, executive clauses also should cover expenses incurred within the normal assigned job location. Again, this is more relevant today as the health care industry consolidates. Expense types included in this section may be automobile, meals and lodging, entertainment, accompanying spouse or family member, telephone, education (including seminars and workshops as well as university-level courses), and credit cards issued to the employee for business expenses. Also included are the following: advances, direct billing, expense reports, and when and if prior approval is required.[33]

Retirement Plan

A retirement or deferred compensation plan is key to any executive compensation plan. If the organization is for-profit, inquire about 401(k) plans and employee matching or discretionary contributions. If the organization is nonprofit, a 403(b) plan with matching or discretionary contributions by the employer may be an option. Language permitting the employee to designate that a portion of her or his salary be put into tax-sheltered investments as deferred income is another option.

An important criterion of any retirement plan is the concept of ownership, or the vesting of the employer's contribution by the employee either immediately or after a minimum of one year. Also important is the portability of the plan. Can you take it with you easily when you leave?

Read carefully the terms of any professed plan to ensure that your interests are protected.

General Liability Insurance

Given the litigious nature of our society, it is wise to ensure that you are protected by the hospital's general liability insurance policy for all acts done by you in good faith during the course of your duties. For example, an employee sues the hospital and you personally for wrongful discharge. In terminating the employee, you acted in good faith and followed hospital policy but now find you must defend yourself against this allegation. You want to be sure that your employer will cover the associated expenses.

Term of Employment and Continuation Clause

The term of employment should be stated specifically in the contract. Generally speaking, the term should be no less than 1 year and no more than 3. A contract will not guarantee employment for the specified term if there is a breach by either party or if there is a "for-cause termination."

Assuming the contract negotiated is satisfactory to both parties and protects their interests, a clause permitting renewal without having to negotiate the entire document may be desirable. For example, a contract that provides a 1-year term should provide that it be automatically renewed on the same terms and conditions unless notice of intention to terminate is given by the specified date prior to the annual renewal/ termination date. For example:

> Should (party) elect not to renew this contract at the end of the term, ninety (90) days written notice shall be given to (the other party to the agreement).[34]

Exclusion of Any Oral Amendments, Termination Clause, and Severance Compensation and Outplacement Support

A severance agreement is a valuable and negotiable benefit for the nurse executive in transition. More than ever before, nurse executives are finding themselves in job situations that lack security and stability.[35] It is important that, whenever possible, nurse executives ensure their security before they are fired or forced to leave their position because of political pressure.[36]

The ideal time to negotiate a security clause is at the time of employment because you have the advantage of being in a position of strength if you are the employer's first choice for the job. However, even if termination is imminent or has already occurred, you may still have a strong position for an equitable severance agreement.

In her article "Negotiating a Severance Agreement," Fisher offers the following counsel:

> Clauses you should request include severance pay. You should receive a minimum of three months pay in your severance package but payment for six months to one year is not uncommon. The pay package can be given in a lump sum or installments. A lump sum can be invested and earn substantial interest that would not be enjoyed with the installment method, while installments may help severed executives better manage their finances. Severance pay, like regular payroll income, is subject to withholding taxes. You may wish to seek the counsel of a tax consultant or financial planner.
>
> The company may try to limit severance pay to a particular time period or the date of your reemployment, whichever is less. Payment should be for the full period negotiated regardless of when you are re-employed. Even if you are fortunate enough to find a great job right away, that severance benefit should still be yours. You have earned it through your pain, loss, and inconvenience. Further, you should request a clause stating severance pay should be continued

and available to the next-of-kin in the unfortunate event that you should die before all payments are made.

Earned bonuses should also be addressed in the severance agreement. Employment may be terminated before the end of a bonus period. Since a bonus is not usually given before work and performance specifications are completed, you may not receive your earned pro rata share unless it is specified in writing. Some companies may time terminations to avoid paying large bonuses. The special skills of an employment law attorney may be required to successfully negotiate in your favor and this is best done at the time the agreement is written.

Disbursement of earned benefit time should be addressed in the agreement. While it seems logical that you would be entitled to all earned and accrued vacation, some companies try to include that time in the three or six months severance offered in their proposal. You should negotiate for full vacation pay. Likewise, if you work for a company with a flexible benefit plan, negotiate payment of part or all of accrued sick leave and personal leave pay.

Insurance benefits are another key component of a severance agreement. You may be entitled to insurance benefits at group rates for up to 18 months after termination under the Consolidated Omnibus Budget Reconciliation Act of 1986 (COBRA, PL 99-272, Sec. 1001). This applies if you were not terminated for gross misconduct and if your employer is covered by the Act. Employers with more than 20 employees working at any time must comply with this law and notify terminated employees of this benefit. The employer may charge you up to 102% of the group rate. You could negotiate for company payment of the premiums for the full time period specified for your severance payments.

Letters of recommendation will be critical to your success in finding new employment. Negotiate to control the content of all letters of recommendation that are written by your employer. A clause in the agreement stating that you will provide such a letter, or that you and the employer must agree on the content of such a letter, will protect you. A statement in the agreement that the company will be held legally liable for detrimental or false information given will have a chilling effect on such negative behavior.

Out-placement services will help you find new employment and thus are important to secure your professional future. These services may include career counseling, resume preparation services, psychological testing, office space, secretarial services, telephone privileges, and coaching on interview skills. Executives most often receive such services through professional out-placement agencies. If you have had a previous positive experience with a particular agency, request that agency specifically. However, most companies contract with a specific agency and may not allow optional service providers.

The severance agreement should specify the duration that the out-placement service will be provided as opposed to specifying a monetary limitation. Out-placement services that continue throughout the entire period of unemployment are preferable to a limited number of visits, a limited period of time, or a specific dollar amount. When the service starts is also vital because you need to start your job search quickly. Quickly starting your search serves two valuable purposes: (a) it allows you to positively turn your vision and actions to the future, and (b) it gets you reemployed faster.

Payment for professional meetings related to the job search may also help with early re-employment. Ask the employer to pay for a "networking" trip to the American Organization of Nurse Executives (AONE) convention or another professional meeting that might yield valuable job contacts and interviews. This opportunity may provide the link that makes a real difference in your job search.[37]

Fisher also advises that you avoid, or control (if avoidance is not possible), certain limitations the company will attempt to impose on your activity once your employment ceases.[38] For example, the company will seek to prevent disclosure of proprietary information such as colleagues' telephone numbers, the number of hospital beds in service, or other information that is not widely known. *Proprietary* refers to any information specific to the corporation or company that does not reside in the public domain. Better language would limit only disclosure of confidential information. The more defined, the less restrictive this clause will be for you.

The employer also may try to limit your contact with employees remaining at the company. Make sure that any such restrictive language specifically indicates the intent of the clause. For example, the company may well be within its rights to limit any actions on your part that would be harmful to itself or individuals but cannot invade your privacy by restricting general socializations with friends and former colleagues.

Finally, the company will present a clause prohibiting your filing a complaint or lawsuit related to either your termination or any other grievance arising from your employment. Such language often specifies various civil rights acts and applicable state statutes. This clause is the payback to the company for the severance agreement and may be unavoidable. However, it is advisable to have legal counsel evaluate the wording. Specifically, retain the right to sue for any malicious actions that arise subsequent to your severance agreement. This is vital if you fear reprisal that might prevent your future reemployment.

Finally, Fisher advises the nurse executive to expect the following provisions to be included as a matter of legal form.[39] The company will want to avoid possible future legal claims, so you should expect a clause stating that the company did not improperly cause the termination but that it was reached by mutual agreement. This is standard language, but specific wording should be reviewed by your attorney.

A clause prohibiting disclosure of the terms of the agreement or circumstances surrounding the termination is standard in all severance packages. Failure to comply with this clause usually invokes penalties such as the threat of legal action or stopping severance payments.

And a clause describing the binding nature of the agreement will be included in agreement. This clause may be written from the standpoint of holding you and your heirs to the terms of the agreement, and also may include language binding the company and future executives to carry out the contract's intent. Such a clause also would state that the contract cannot be changed through oral agreements.

Illness

Another issue you may wish to consider including in the contract is the effect of employee illness on the contract. Although a temporary illness does not give the employer the right to terminate the contract, a prolonged illness that materially affects the employee's ability to perform his or her duties may cause the employee to be in breach unless otherwise protected. A provision such as the following offers some protection:

> If the Employee is terminated for disability, then, in addition to any other benefits to which the Employee may become entitled, the Employer agrees to pay the sum of (amount) per month commencing with the first month after termination and ending with the month in which the Employee's death occurs or with the Employee's return to full-time work by performing substantially of the same quality and under the same terms and condition as prior to any disability.[40]

Death of the employee terminates the contract as a matter of law.[41]

Restrictive Covenants

Restrictive covenants are used in a number of fields to prohibit an employee from working for a competing employer or starting a competing business, or to protect against disclosure of confidential information, trade secrets, customer solicitation, employee solicitation, and inventions.

Employers cannot prevent former employees from competing with them unless they are bound by enforceable restrictive covenants. For restrictive covenants to be enforceable, they must be:

1. Reasonably limited in scope to time, place, and activities
2. Designed to protect a legitimate employer interest
3. Supported by valid consideration
4. Not harmful to the public and
5. Ancillary to some other agreement because a contract cannot restrain competition as its sole or primary purpose; that is, an agreement containing a covenant not to compete must have a purpose other than restricting competition involving employment or the sale of a business.[42]

Often restricted is the geographical area where similar employment may be sought. Time limitations also are included to restrict the employee's ability to use information gained from the former employer. Subject matter usually covered by these covenants also includes the employee's commitment not to compete with the former employer for a specified time within a specified geographical territory. The employee may not use or disclose customer lists, information, data, or trade secrets learned during employment. Additionally, clauses granting the employer sale rights to inventions, products, and information developed during employment may be included. The reasonableness of the covenant is determined by reviewing the employer interest sought to be protected. Generally, the employer's need for protection is balanced against the hardship imposed on the employee by limiting his or her employment opportunities.[43]

The matter of restrictive covenants may not be of great concern to the nurse executive, as provisions of this type more easily apply outside the health care sector. However, in today's fiercely competitive environment, the nurse executive should avoid any attempt by the employer to restrict his or her employment future. Defense of the reasonableness of the restrictive covenant falls to the employer, but the nurse executive in a new position does not want to be placed in the position of having to defend an allegation of breach of a restrictive covenant.

The desire to restrict may occur if the nurse executive has a relationship with key members of the staff who may follow him or her, taking large pieces of the business with them if the nurse executive leaves to work for another health care system in the region. The issue may arise as well if the nurse invented or perfected some product or process while in the employment of the company. The company may seek to own that invention and any profits flowing from it.

Another way in which a restrictive covenant may be advanced by the employer is by limiting the nurse executive's pursuit of outside business concerns that might impair his or her full-time efforts on the job or be in competition with the organization while in the employment of the organization. For example, the ability to write books or articles or to teach part-time at the local college or university may be opportunities the nurse executive wishes to reserve for him- or herself.

In summary, although the matter of restrictive covenants is largely uncharted territory for health care executives, you must always be alert to protect your own interests and vigorously defend against any encroachment on your future freedoms and rights.

Miscellaneous Considerations

Miscellaneous clauses or considerations to be addressed on a case-by-case basis include:

- Relocation expenses
- Fringe benefits
- Alternative dispute resolution mechanisms
- Cleanup
- Remedies
- Governing law
- Assignment
- Notice
- Entire agreement
- Separability
- Signatures

Relocation Expenses

If relocation is required, you should include reimbursement for the specific expenses involved. It is to your advantage to have the terms itemized rather than using the term "all reasonable moving expenses." Use of a relocation service for the sale of your present home and closing costs on a new home could be included. General moving expenses, in addition to the moving company expense, can include clauses for packing and unpacking household items, temporary living expenses during the relocation, mileage to drive vehicles from the old to new locations, trip expenses to look for new housing, and other miscellaneous costs of actually moving the family.

Fringe Benefits

In the case of mergers or acquisitions, an acquired company will have a different fringe package from the acquiring company. To the extent possible, you should try to ensure that the better benefit package will apply to your employment where the matter is not otherwise addressed in the contract.

Alternative Dispute Resolution Mechanisms

The requirement to use alternate dispute resolution procedures such as arbitration may be incorporated into employment contracts. In this way, disputes arising out of or under the contract can be resolved without resorting to the judicial forum. These procedures may be quicker and less expensive and may avoid publicity because they are usually private.[44]

Most states have enacted some form of the Uniform Arbitration Act,[45] which legalizes written agreements requiring arbitration of future disputes, including disputes arising out of employment contracts. To be enforceable, the arbitration agreement must bind both employee and employer to arbitrate the dispute.[46]

The employee must carefully consider an arbitration clause's desirability. Even though arbitration offers advantages regarding expense and speed, he or she may have to forego the advantage of a jury trial in which sympathizers favor the employee. Sympathetic juries often make larger awards than administrative law judges in charge of the arbitration process.

Arbitration agreements often represent a compromise based on the parties' bargaining strength, political considerations, and other practical needs. The contract's arbitration clause can make arbitration either advisory or binding on the parties. Likewise, its use can be limited to just certain contract disputes or expanded to cover any and all contract disputes.

In drafting the arbitration clause, care should be taken to limit the extent to which disputes are to be arbitrated, as well as the arbitrator's authority. The clause should provide that the arbitrator cannot amend, modify, nullify, ignore, or add to the agreement's provisions. The arbitrator's sole task is to determine whether a particular pattern of conduct constitutes a contract violation. He or she applies the existing contract to the dispute's facts to determine whether a violation has occurred.[47]

An important clause of the arbitration agreement involves deciding how to allocate the expenses. Costs may be divided equally between the parties or the losing party may pay all of them.[48]

Cleanup

If the agreement is not used for the first term of employment but, instead, is used to continue a relationship that already may have started, the new contract should have a "cleanup" clause stating that it supersedes and takes the place of all prior agreements.[49]

Remedies

Remedies for breach of the agreement may not only include termination of the agreement but also require payment for damages. For example, if the employer breaches the agreement by terminating the nurse executive without cause 2 years into a 3-year agreement, a remedy clause in the original agreement might require the employer to continue the nurse's salary and benefits until the end of the 3-year term. Thus, the nurse executive is protected in the event of breach.[50]

Governing Law

A clause identifying which jurisdiction's laws will apply in interpreting and enforcing the contract is important because state laws vary widely. With more and more health care systems crossing state lines, resolving this matter in the contract can avoid later costly and lengthy resolution in the courts.

Sample clauses follow:

Governing Law—Basic

This agreement shall be interpreted in accordance with, and the rights of the Employee and Employer shall be determined by, the laws of (state's name).[51]

Governing Law—State

This agreement shall be governed in all respects and be interpreted by and under the laws of (state's name), except to the extent that this law may be preempted by applicable federal law, including regulations, opinions, or orders duly issued by (Federal Agency's name) under the (Federal statutes), in which event this Agreement shall be governed and be interpreted by and under this federal law.[52]

Assignment

Generally, the employee or the employer each may assign or transfer all rights and benefits under an employment contract. However, the employee cannot transfer his or her obligation under the contract to perform duties involving his or her personal ability, integrity, or responsibility.

Assignment clauses are particularly useful when the employer sells its business, because they permit the employment relationship to continue uninterrupted. Likewise, if the contract contains a clause allowing the restrictive covenant to be transferred to the benefit of the new employer, it may be. Without this clause, a restrictive covenant may not be automatically assignable.[53]

Sample clauses follow:

Assignment—Basic

This Agreement shall be binding upon the Employee's and the Employer's respective heirs, successors, and assigns.

Assignment — Comprehensive

This Agreement shall be binding upon and inure to the benefit of the Employee and the Employer and their respective heirs, successors, assigns, legal representatives, executors, and administrators.[54]

Notice

Certain provisions of the employment contract may require notice to be given by the employee or the employer. Resignation and termination provisions generally require this notice. An additional clause should specifically set forth how, when, and where notice should be given and describe how it is to be given. The notice clause should be included to eliminate any confusion, pinpoint responsibility, and indicate where notices should be sent.[55]

Include in the notice clause employer and employee addresses, the type of notice usually written, and mailing/sending instructions.

Entire Agreement

To strengthen the employment contract's terms, a clause should provide that there are no other oral or written agreements covering the contract's terms and conditions, and that the contract controls the employment relationship. Should a dispute arise, this provision will prevent employee and employer from introducing other documents or outside evidence different from the contract's terms.[56]

The following examples should be considered for use as the "entire agreement" clause in employment contracts:

Entire Agreement — Basic

This Agreement constitutes the complete understanding between the parties, all prior representations or agreements having been merged into this Agreement.

Entire Agreement — Comprehensive

This Agreement sets forth the understanding and agreement between the parties and shall be binding upon the parties and their respective successors, heirs, and assigns. All prior negotiations, agreements, and understandings are superseded hereby.[57]

Separability Clause

A separability clause should be included in the employment contract to retain the contract's enforceability should litigation arise concerning a particular section of the contract. This clause preserves the remaining portions of the employment contract's clauses should one or more clauses or their parts be found invalid. It is especially useful when litigation arises over restrictive covenants.[58]

A sample clause follows:

Separability—Basic

If any provision, paragraph, or subparagraph of this Agreement is adjudged by any court to be void or unenforceable in whole or in part, this adjudication shall not affect the validity of the remainder of the Agreement, including any other provision, paragraph, or subparagraph. Each provision, paragraph, and subparagraph of this Agreement is separable from every other provision, paragraph, and subparagraph, and constitutes a separate and distinct covenant.[59]

Signatures

A contract is not valid without a signature clause and the signatures of both employer and employee. Many examples exist in case law of litigation over contracts that were never signed.[60] A sample long-form contract, including most of the clauses described here, is provided in the appendix.

Common Questions and Answers

Following are some common questions that people have about job loss. The answers provided encapsulate much of the information in this chapter.

- *Why should I request a written employment contract from my new employer? Isn't the company's word good enough?* As health care becomes increasingly complex and chaotic, nurse executives frequently are placed in vulnerable, even risky, situations. By documenting the expectations of the job and terms and conditions of your employment, you provide increased security for yourself in the event of changed circumstances. With high executive turnover, downsizing, and consolidations, the individual who negotiates your employment may very well be gone if questions about the terms of your employment arise. Further, a written employment contract lessens the likelihood that you will be terminated on some arbitrary point and secures your personal circumstances if you find yourself suddenly unemployed.
- *What options do I have if my employer refuses to agree to a written employment contract?* In this eventuality, keep pressing as diplomatically as possible, suggesting, at the least, use of a memorandum or letter of agreement. If the employer flatly refuses any type of written agreement, you must decide whether the proposed compensation is adequate to assume the potential risks of the position. You may want to consider withdrawing from negotiations.
- *What type of information should I learn about my future employer before negotiating a contract, and how can I obtain it?* It is important that you understand your prospective employer's professional and personal interests before you enter into negotiations. Professionally, you must ascertain the organization's objectives in securing your employment, current organizational policies or pay practices, what limitations (if any) have been placed on the negotiations, and whether other employment contracts will be modeled after this one, making it precedent setting. Personally, you should determine as much as you can about the prospective employer in order to better understand his or her approach to problem solving and management style. You can then design your approach to negotiations to address the needs of the organization and the personality of the individual employer.

  This type of information can be obtained in a number of ways. In addition to requesting copies of all relevant policies and practices, listen carefully for inferences from not only the prospective employer but also current employees of the organization with whom you may speak during the interview process. Contact colleagues who may have knowledge or insights about the prospective employer. Try to determine his or her reputation in the professional community.

- *How can I be a strong negotiator without appearing to be demanding and inflexible?* In general, a professional relationship is not damaged by tough negotiations. Although your behavior must be professional, objective, and unemotional at all times, you should resist the temptation to be submissive for fear of jeopardizing your future relationship with your boss. If you allow yourself to be taken advantage of, you will feel angry with yourself for giving in and you may feel resentful toward your new employer. Instead, identify and prioritize your interests prior to negotiations and consider multiple ways of addressing your needs. In this way, you can offer your employer choices and appear reasonable and flexible.

- *What are principled negotiations, and how should I go about encouraging this type of process rather than traditional adversarial negotiations?* *Principled negotiations* are those that decide issues on their merits rather than through a process focused only on what each side desires. Through principled negotiations, both parties look for mutual gains wherever possible, and when interests conflict, results are based on some fair standard independent of the will of either side. An example of this standard might be basing a compensation package on the Hay Hospital Compensation Survey. This process attempts to reduce the adversarial nature of traditional negotiations. You can encourage principled negotiations by becoming familiar with the techniques described by Ury and Fisher.[61] By employing these techniques yourself, you can set the tone and standard for the process.

- *Does an employment contract have to be written to be enforceable?* An employment contract does not necessarily have to be written to be binding, but without documenting the contract in writing, the terms and conditions offered and accepted may be unclear or misunderstood. If there is disagreement over the terms, the will of the player in power—the employer—is most likely to prevail without additional costly and time-consuming legal action.

- *Is it necessary to have an attorney review my employment contract before I sign it? What about an offer letter or letter of intent?* Although not absolutely necessary, it is highly advisable to have an attorney review your formal employment contract before it is signed. Your prospective employer has most likely had it reviewed by legal counsel to protect the interests of the organization; thus, you should obtain the same protection for your interests. Offer letters and letters of intent, especially if lengthy or complex, also should be reviewed by legal counsel. Even more important would be review of the proposed response to these letters to ensure that your interests are protected.

- *How can I determine whether the salary I am being offered is equitable?* You need to determine whether the compensation being offered is similar to compensations for like positions in your region of the country. The Hay Hospital Compensation Survey is one means of obtaining this type of information. Job directories in professional journals also can be helpful in establishing a salary range. Finally, networking with colleagues in similar positions may help you identify an acceptable range.

- *How long should the term of employment be defined in my employment contract?* Commonly, the term should be no less than 1 year and no more than 3. You also may include a clause permitting renewal without having to renegotiate the entire document. A contract that provides a 1-year term should stipulate that it is automatically renewed on the same terms and conditions unless notice of intention to terminate is given by a specified date prior to the annual renewal date.

- *My employment contract does not guarantee employment if there is a "for-cause termination." What exactly is this?* A *for-cause termination* is one that the employer can justify with sufficient legal reasons so as to prevail should he or she choose to claim wrongful discharge or breach of contract. Violation of employer policy, documented performance issues with employee notification and subsequent failure to correct, or employee breach of the employment contract may provide sufficient justification for for-cause termination.

- *If I am terminated without an employment contract, can I still negotiate a severance agreement?* Although the ideal time to negotiate a severance package is at the time of employment, you still may be able to negotiate one at the time of termination. If the termination is for cause, however, there is little hope of negotiating a severance agreement. But if the termination occurred for other reasons, such as political maneuvering or downsizing, appealing to the employer's sense of justice or guilt may be an effective strategy. In the latter instance, the employer may believe it is in his or her best interest not to have you leave angry with litigation on your mind.

- *Does a severance agreement need to be reviewed by an attorney if it is not included in a formal employment contract?* Legal review is always advisable to protect your interests. It does not matter how an employment arrangement is packaged, the same issues arise. Legal review ensures that all agreements affecting your employment, whatever their form, protect your interests.

References

1. American College of Hospital Administrators. Contracts for hospital chief executive officers. In: *Report of the Ad Hoc Committee on Contracts for Hospital Chief Executive Officers.* Chicago: ACHA, 1982, p. 8.

2. Eubanks, P. Boards, execs more savvy about CEO contracts. *Hospitals* 66(4):66, Feb. 20, 1992.

3. Blouin, A. S., and Brent, N. J. Nurse administrators in job transition. *Journal of Nursing Administration* 22(1):10, Jan. 1992.

4. Tarrant, J. *Perks and Parachutes.* New York City: The Stonesony Press, 1985, p. 59.

5. Tarrant, p. 61.

6. Fisher, R., and Ury, W. *Getting to Yes: Negotiating Agreement without Giving In* Boston: Houghton Mifflin, 1983, p. xi.

7. Tarrant, p. 76.

8. Fisher and Ury, p. 51.

9. Tarrant, p. 75.

10. Fisher and Ury, p. 42.

11. Fisher and Ury, p. xii.

12. Fisher, R., and Brown, S. *Getting Together: Building Relationships as We Negotiate.* New York City: Penguin Books, 1988.

13. Fisher and Ury, p. 12.

14. *Hay Hospital Compensation Survey.* Philadelphia: The Hay Group and American Society for Healthcare Human Resources Adminstration, 1995.

15. Fisher and Ury, p. 10.

16. Fisher and Brown, p. xiii.

17. Decker, K. H., and Felix, H. T., II. *Drafting and Revising Employment Contracts.* New York City: John Wiley and Sons, 1991, pp. 23–24.

18. Hancock, W. A., editor. *The Lawyer's Brief.* Chesterfield, OH: Business Laws, Inc., 1981, p. 3.

19. Decker and Felix, pp. 28–29.

20. Trandel-Korenchuk, K. M., and Trandel-Korenchuk, D. M. Legal forum. *Nursing Administration Quarterly* 13(4):62, Summer 1989.

21. Trandel-Korenchuk and Trandel-Korenchuk, p. 62.

22. Hay Hospital Compensation Survey.

23. Boyer, R., and Savageau, D. *Places Rated.* New York City: Rand McNally, 1993.

24. Hindle, T. *Field Guide to Business Terms.* Boston: Harvard Business School Press, 1993, p. 205.

25. Tarrant, p. 125.

26. Decker and Felix, p. 78.

27. Decker and Felix, p. 90.

28. Decker and Felix, p. 91.

29. Decker and Felix, p. 91.

30. Decker and Felix, p. 93.

31. Decker and Felix, p. 95.

32. Decker and Felix, p. 97.

33. Decker and Felix, pp. 100–101.

34. Witt, J. A. *Contracts for Health Care Executives.* Oakbrook, IL: Witt Associates, 1984, p. 5.

35. Fisher, M. L. Negotiating a severance agreement. *Nursing Economics* 9(1):36, Jan.–Feb. 1991.

36. Fisher, p. 36.

37. Fisher, p. 37. Quoted with permission.

38. Fisher, p. 38.

39. Fisher, p. 39.

40. Decker and Felix, p. 140.

41. Buccini v. Paterno Constru. Co., 253 N.Y. 256, 170 N.E. 910 (1930); Sargent v. McLeod, 209 N.Y. 360, 103 N.E. 164 (1913); Segar v. King Features Syndicate, 262 App. Div. 221, 28 N.Y.S. 2d 542 (1st Dep't. 1941) aff'd. 289 N.Y. 579, 43 N.E. 2d 717 (1942); George v. Richards, 361 Pa. 278, 64 A.2d 811 (1949). See also 6 Williston, Contracts, sections 1940, 1941 (rev. ed. 1938).

42. Decker and Felix, p. 105.

43. Decker and Felix, p. 106.

44. Decker and Felix, p. 141.

45. Uniform Arbitration Act (1988).

46. Decker and Felix, p. 141.

47. Decker and Felix, p. 143.

48. Decker and Felix, p. 143.

49. Hancock, p. 23.
50. Decker and Felix, p. 152.
51. Decker and Felix, p. 156.
52. Decker and Felix, p. 156.
53. Decker and Felix, p. 156.
54. Decker and Felix, p. 157.
55. Decker and Felix, p. 157.
56. Decker and Felix, p. 159.
57. Decker and Felix, p. 160.
58. Decker and Felix, p. 160.
59. Decker and Felix, p. 161.
60. Decker and Felix, p. 161.
61. Ury and Fisher, p. xii.

Bibliography

Alexander, J., and Brooks, D. C. New dimensions in board–CEO relations. *Trustee* 39(6):24–27, 1986.

Allen, J., editor. *The Employee Termination Handbook.* New York City: John Wiley and Sons, 1986.

American Academy of Medical Directors. *Physician Managers and the Law: Employment and Personal Service Contracts.* Tampa: AAMD, 1987.

American College of Healthcare Executives. *Contracts for Healthcare Executives.* Chicago: Foundation of the American College of Healthcare Executives, 1987.

American College of Hospital Administrators. *Contracts for Hospital Chief Executive Officers.* Chicago: ACHA, 1982.

Averill, J. Health care reform and hospital downsizing: facing new realities (letter). *Hospitals and Health Networks* 67(24):8, Dec. 20, 1993.

Benton-Powers, S. Minimizing termination liability: negotiating employee resignations. *Healthcare Newsletter* 1(3):1, 1991.

Biordi, D. L., and Garsiner, D. The handwriting on the wall: warning signs of impending job loss. *Journal of Nursing Administration* 22(11):15–20, 1992.

Blouin, A. S., and Brent, N. J. The chief nurse executive and intellectual property law: selected concerns. *Journal of Nursing Administration* 24(4):21-23, Apr. 1994.

Blouin, A. S., and Brent, N. J. Nurse administrators in job transition: stories from the front. *Journal of Nursing Administration* 22(12):13-14, 27, Dec. 1992.

Buyse, M., and Falcao-Blumenfeld, P. Negotiating contracts. *Journal of American Medical Women's Association* 46(3):75-76, 82, May-June 1991.

Decker, K., and Felix, H. T. *Drafting and Revising Employment Contracts*. New York City: John Wiley and Sons, 1991.

Dolan, R. C. Breaking down the barriers to employment contracts. *Healthcare Executive* 2(5):60, Sept.-Oct. 1987.

Employment contracts bill. *New Zealand Nursing Journal* 84(2):10-11, Mar. 1991.

Eubanks, P. Boards, execs more savvy about CEO contracts. *Hospitals* 66(4):66, Feb. 20, 1992.

Eubanks, P. CEO pay: public scrutiny and pay for performance are the new ground rules. *Hospitals* 66(12):22, 24, June 20, 1992.

Eubanks, P. Contract-management careers: risks, rewards. *Hospitals* 66(21):68, Nov. 5, 1992.

Fisher, M. Negotiating a severance agreement. *Nursing Economics* 9(1):36-39, 1991.

Fisher, R., and Ury, W. *Getting to Yes: Negotiating Agreement without Giving In*. Boston: Houghton Mifflin, 1983

Freeman, C. K. Administrator employment contracts. Denver: Medical Group Management Association, 1989.

Greene, J. Lutheran General selling contracts to execs (news). *Modern Healthcare* 23(31):8, Aug. 2, 1993.

Harnden, L. Employment contracts reduce employers' liability. *Dimensions in Health Service* 64(7):33, Oct. 1987.

Hauser, M. C. Attracting top candidates in troubled times. *Hospitals* 65(12):60, June 20, 1991.

Hewitt Associates. *Executive Severance Arrangements.* Lincolnshire, IL: Hewitt Associates, 1991.

Ireson, C., and Weaver, D. Marketing nursing beyond the walls. *Journal of Nursing Administration* 22(1):57–60, Jan. 1992.

Johnsson, J. CEO firings: the medical staff's key role. *Hospitals* 64(4):70, Feb. 20, 1990.

Johnsson, J. CEO firings: warning signs of unhappy boards. *Hospitals* 65(19):56, Oct. 5, 1991.

Korenchuk, K. M., and Hunting, S. R. Physician employment contracts and restrictive covenants. *North Carolina Medical Journal* 50(11):631–33, Nov. 1989.

Lampert, J., and Bjork, D. Annual survey: executive compensation under fire. *Hospitals* 66(17):24–28, 30, 32, Sept. 5, 1992.

Moore, T. F. Executive contracts from the board's perspective. *Michigan Hospitals* 26(4):57, Apr. 1990.

Moran, E. J. Fired CEOs: how to tackle the job interview. *Hospitals* 64(19):72, Oct. 5, 1990.

Moran, E. J. Merger aftermath: can your job be saved? *Hospitals* 64(13):82, July 5, 1990.

Noyes, B. J. Contract management. Filling the void created by CNE vacancies. *Journal of Nursing Administration* 22(10):21–24, Oct. 1992.

Roper, R. R. Restrictive covenants in professional employment contracts. *American Journal of Roentgenology* 153(5):1089–90, Nov. 1989.

Rozovsky, L. E., and Rozovsky, F. A. Why employment contracts for CEOs should be considered. *Health Care* 31(2):30, Mar. 1989.

Simpson, R. L. What you need to know about negotiating contracts. *Nursing Management* 22(9):22–23, Sept. 1991.

Sovereign, K. *Personnel Law.* 2nd ed. Englewood Cliffs, NJ: Prentice-Hall, 1989.

Tarrant, J. *Perks and Parachutes.* New York City: The Stonesony Press, 1985.

The Lawyer's Brief. *Corporate Counsel's Primer on Employment Contracts.* Chesterfield, OH: Business Laws, 1981.

Thompson, H. A. Restrictive covenants. *Texas Medicine* 86(1):60–61, Jan. 1990.

Trandel-Korenchuk, D. M., and Trandel-Korenchuk, K. M. Legal forum: the employee contract. *Nursing Administration Quarterly* 13(4):61–65, Summer 1989.

Ward, S. F. If you're hiring or job hunting, how to deal with exec recruiters. *OR Manager* 4(8):4–5, Aug. 1988.

Wieland, J. B., and Homer, L. C. Law and legal concepts. Contracts of employment. *Topics in Health Care Finance* 10(4):16–27, Summer 1984.

Witt Associates Inc. *Today's Nurse Executive: Report of a Survey.* Oakbrook, IL: Witt Associates Inc., 1990.

Appendix.   Sample Contract for a Nurse Executive

This agreement, made and effective as of the _____ day of _____, 19_____, between (Name of Hospital), (City, State), and (Name of Individual), (City, State).

WHEREAS, (Name of Hospital), desires to secure the services of (Name of Individual) for _____ years from the effective date of this contract and (Name of Individual) desires to accept such employment.

NOW, THEREFORE, in consideration of the material advantages accruing to the two parties and the mutual covenants contained herein, (Name of Hospital), (hereafter called the Hospital), and (Name of Individual) (hereafter called Name of Individual), agree with each other as follows:

(Name of Individual) will render full-time professional services to the Hospital in the capacity of Chief Nursing Executive of the Hospital corporation for the _____ year term of this contract. She will at all times, faithfully, industriously, and to the best of her ability, perform all duties that may be required of her by virtue of her position as Chief Nursing Executive and all duties set forth in Hospital bylaws to the reasonable satisfaction of the Chief Executive Officer. Her duties shall specifically include:

1. Ensure optimal and efficient medical services to patients by coordinating medical expertise with the medical staff in the areas of new ventures and service issues.
2. Assure effective and efficient operation by developing, directing, coordinating, and maintaining the activities of the Nursing Division.
3. Increase the hospital's emphasis on patient quality by implementing principles of quality and total quality management.
4. Contribute to the financial viability of Hospital by developing and implementing a comprehensive financial plan for the Nursing Division and by training managers to be effective financial managers.
5. Assure high-quality patient care, protection of patient rights, and compliance with applicable regulations and standards by developing appropriate and effective policies and procedures.
6. Provide a constructive work environment at Hospital by acting as a change agent and assisting with the implementation of an appropriate organizational culture.
7. Contribute to the ongoing operations of Hospital by representing nursing care during JCAHO accreditation inspections.
8. Assure a qualified and motivated staff to meet the needs of the department by overseeing the selection, training development, and ongoing coaching of the Nursing staff.
9. Assure overall smooth operations by coordinating and integrating the activities of Hospital with other hospitals under the corporate umbrella.

In addition, she shall perform in the same manner any special duties assigned or delegated to her by the Chief Executive Officer of Hospital.

(Continued on next page)

Appendix   (Continued)

Page 2

Evaluation
The Chief Executive Officer of Hospital, after six months and annually
thereafter, shall evaluate (Name of Individual)'s performance as Chief Nursing
Executive. Evaluation shall be based on performance of duties listed above and
achievement of mutually agreed-to management goals using the evaluation tool
appended to this agreement.

Salary
In consideration for these services as Chief Nursing Executive, the Hospital
agrees to pay (Name of Individual) $_____ per annum or such higher
figure as shall be agreed upon at an annual review of her compensation by the
Hospital Chief Executive Officer. This annual review shall occur three months
prior to the end of each year of the contract for the express purpose of considering increments. The amount of $_____ shall be payable in equal
monthly installments throughout the contract year, beginning _____.
(Name of Individual) may, at her option, require that such portion of said
salary as she may designate be put into tax-sheltered investments as deferred
income.

Bonus Program
The Employer shall make the Employee a participant in the Executive bonus
program, applicable to the fiscal year ending _____. It is intended
that a similar program will be adopted for subsequent fiscal years, the precise
terms of which will be negotiated between the parties.

Profit Sharing
The Employee shall be eligible to participate in the Employer's profit-sharing
plan as set forth in the Employer's policy as it may exist or be modified from
time to time.

Stock Option
The Employee shall be eligible to participate in the Employer's stock option
plan as set forth in the Employer's policy as it may exist or be modified from
time to time.

Vacation
(Name of Individual) shall be entitled to _____ weeks of compensated
vacation time in each of the contract years, to be taken at times mutually
agreed upon between her and _____. Unused vacation time from
each year may accumulate over the life of this contract. Unused vacation time
will be paid in full at the termination of this agreement.

Appendix   (Continued)

Page 3

Sick Leave
(Name of Individual) shall also be entitled to _____ weeks of compensated sick leave in each contract year, to be taken if required, whenever necessary throughout the year. Sick leave may be accumulated to the extent not used up, to a maximum of _____ days. Unused sick leave will be paid out at 50 percent of dollar value on termination of this agreement.

Disability
In the event of a single period of prolonged inability to work due to the results of a sickness or an injury, (Name of Individual) will be compensated at her full rate of pay for a minimum of _____ months from the date of the sickness or injury.

Meeting Expenses
In addition, (Name of Individual) will be permitted to be absent from the Hospital during working days to attend professional meetings in the United States and elsewhere and to attend such outside professional duties in the hospital field as have been mutually agreed upon between her and the Hospital Chief Executive Officer. Attendance at such approved meetings and accomplishment of approved professional duties shall be fully compensated service time and shall not be considered vacation time. The Hospital shall reimburse (Name of Individual) for all expenses incurred by her and her spouse incident to attendance at approved professional meetings, and such entertainment expenses incurred by (Name of Individual) in furtherance of the Hospital's interests, provided, however, that such reimbursement is approved by the Hospital Chief Executive Officer.

Association Dues
The Hospital agrees to pay dues to professional associations and societies and to such service organizations and clubs of which (Name of Individual) is a member, approved by _____ as being in the best interest of the Hospital.

Insurance
The Hospital also agrees to:

- insure (Name of Individual) under its general liability insurance policy for all acts done by her in good faith as Chief Nursing Executive throughout the term of this contract;
- provide, throughout the term of this contract, a group life insurance policy for (Name of Individual) in an amount equivalent to $50,000 plus three times her annual salary, payable to the beneficiary of her choice;

(Continued on next page)

Appendix   (Continued)

Page 4

- provide comprehensive health and major medical insurance to include dental, vision, mental, and home health services for (Name of Individual) and her family;

Travel and Entertainment Expenses
All travel and entertainment expenses, local and otherwise, related to the business and interests of the Hospital incurred by (Name of Individual) shall be reimbursed by the Hospital. Travel accident insurance covering (Name of Individual) in the sum of $_____ will be purchased.

Other Miscellaneous Benefits
A corporate credit card for use by (Name of Individual) for business expenses will be issued to (Name of Individual) for the term of this agreement.

An automobile, leased or purchased at the beginning of alternate fiscal years, will be furnished for the use of (Name of Individual) and she will be reimbursed for expenses of its operation.

Employer's Option to Terminate
The Employer is granted an option to terminate the Employee's employment, without cause, upon (Time Period) prior written notice to the Employee.

After such termination, all rights, duties, and obligations of both parties shall cease except that the Hospital shall continue to pay (Name of Individual) her then monthly salary for the month in which her duties were terminated and for twenty-four consecutive months thereafter as an agreed-upon termination payment. During this period, (Name of Individual) shall not be required to perform any duties for the Hospital or come to the Hospital. Neither shall the fact that she seeks, accepts, and undertakes other employment during this period affect such payments. Also, for the period during which such payments are being made, the Hospital agrees to keep (Name of Individual)'s group life, disability, health, and major medical insurance coverage paid up and in effect.

Outplacement support will be provided by (Name of Company) for _____ months or until (Name of Individual) accepts new employment.

Should the Hospital in its discretion change (Name of Individual)'s duties so it can reasonably be found that she is no longer performing the duties of the Chief Nursing Executive of the Hospital, (Name of Individual) shall have the right, in her complete discretion, to terminate this contract by written notice delivered to _____. After such termination, all rights, duties, and obligations of both shall cease except that the Hospital shall continue to pay (Name of Individual) her then monthly salary for the month in which her duties

Appendix   (Continued)

Page 5

were terminated and for twenty-four consecutive months thereafter as the agreed-upon termination payment. During this period, (Name of Individual) shall not be required to perform any duties for the Hospital or come to the Hospital. Neither shall the fact that she seeks, accepts, or undertakes other employment during this term affect such payments. Also, for the period during which such payments are being made, the Hospital agrees to keep (Name of Individual)'s group life, disability, health, and major medical insurance coverage paid up and in effect.

Employee's Option to Terminate
Should (Name of Individual) in her discretion elect to terminate this contract for any other reason than as stated, she shall give the (Name of Employer) (Time Period) written notice. At the end of the notice period, all rights, duties, and obligations of both parties to the contract shall cease.

Contract Extension
Negotiations for the extension of this contract, or for agreement on the terms of a new contract, shall be completed, or the decision made not to negotiate a new contract made, not later than the end of the seventh month of the final contract year. By mutual agreement of the parties, this contract and all its terms and conditions may be extended from year to year or for a term beyond its initial term by a simple letter exchanged between the parties at any time during the contract term.

Amendments
Except as otherwise specifically provided, the terms and conditions of this contract may be amended at any time by mutual agreement of the parties, provided that before any amendment shall be valid or effective, it shall have been reduced to writing and signed by (Name of Hospital Representative) and (Name of Individual).

Notice
Written notices to be given under this agreement shall be sent by registered or certified mail, return receipt requested, to the addresses set forth below:

Employee: _____

Employer: _____

(Continued on next page)

Appendix   (Continued)

Page 6

Separability
The invalidity or unenforceability of any particular provision of this contract shall not affect its other provisions, and this contract shall be construed in all respects as if such invalid or unenforceable provision had been omitted.

Assignment
This agreement shall be binding upon and inure to the benefit of the Hospital, its successors, and assigns, and shall be binding upon (Name of Individual), her administrators, executors, legatees, heirs, and assigns.

Governing Law
This agreement shall be governed in all respects and be interpreted by and under the laws of (Name of State), except to the extent that this law may be preempted by applicable federal law, including regulations, opinions, or orders duly issued by (Name of Federal Agency) under the (Federal Statutes), in which event this Agreement shall be governed and be interpreted by and under this federal law.

Entire Agreement
This Agreement contains the entire agreement among the parties, and there are no agreements, representations, or warranties that are not set forth. All prior negotiations, agreements, and understandings are superseded.

Arbitration
Any dispute or disagreement arising out of this Agreement or a claimed breach, except that which involves a right to injunctive relief, shall be resolved by arbitration under the Voluntary Labor Arbitration Rules of the American Arbitration Association. The arbitrator's decisions shall be final and binding upon the parties and judgment may be entered in any court.

This contract is signed this _____ day of _____, 19_____.

(Name of Hospital)

BY: _____
(Hospital Representative)

WITNESS: _____

_____
(Name of Individual)

WITNESS: _____

Note: This contract was reprinted with permission from the American College of Hospital Administration, Chicago, IL.

Chapter 5

Managing the Trauma
of Involuntary Termination:
A Case Study

Deborah A. Yancer, MS, RN, and Julie Klausen Moe, RN

Mary Davis (a fictitious name) was a nurse executive in progressively responsible roles for 15 years. She had been a consistently high performer and was well respected in her employing organization as well as the nursing field. This chapter consists of excerpts from her private journal that offer snapshots of an executive experiencing involuntary termination. Each excerpt is followed by a commentary written by the authors to provide reflection on Mary's experience and reactions and to apply the principles described throughout this book. This case study offers readers personal insight into job loss and the strategies necessary to transform it into a successful career transition.

Day 1

Today was my first day back to work from a great vacation. The morning began as all first days back do—busy catching up and making great progress at that. While I was on the phone, I overheard my secretary in conversation with my boss at her desk just outside my door. They were arranging for an appointment that afternoon for him to "catch me up on things." Not at all unusual, until I heard him say that the meeting would be in his boss's office—very unusual!

I went to the meeting expecting bad news. With all the changes that have resulted from the recent consolidation, there was tension throughout the organization. However, I was not prepared to hear that for political reasons I could no longer be successful in this organization. The reasons were vague, and, in some cases, contrived. Given the situation, we agreed that I would leave the organization. My superiors communicated their disappointment, their realization that I was a scapegoat in this situation, and their support for me in transition.

I cried. I searched my brain for all I had ever read about how you manage these situations. But there was nothing that could have prepared me for the shock I felt. How could one of the highest-performing executives, somebody who was recently promoted, become of no value to an organization so easily? I tried to compose myself and at one point sobbed uncontrollably as the finality of the situation hit me. Concern for myself, my family, and my colleagues flooded my mind. How would people understand and accept this? How could I survive this?

Eventually, we agreed that it would be best that I go home for the day. Arrangements were made to bring my briefcase and car keys. My boss drove me to my car. I don't remember much about the drive to the parking lot or the drive away from the hospital. I do remember the sun was shining brightly and everything seemed normal — but me.

I called my husband on my cellular phone. I told him something awful had happened and I needed him to meet me somewhere. I was crying. I knew I could not go home, it was summertime and the children were at home. I needed help right away to deal with what had happened and to determine what to do next.

We met at a restaurant. It was early afternoon, so very few people were there. I recounted the entire conversation for him. We agreed on two actions that day—we would not tell our children until we had a clearer idea of the situation, and I would call a recruiter I knew and seek advice. I did not go home until much later that day—so things would seem normal. You see, executives rarely come home early, especially the first day back from vacation, unless they have lost their job.

Commentary

Although Mary was aware there was tension in the organization, she was not aware that she was in any personal danger. Chapter 1 discusses typical warning signs observed in organizations when a manager's job is at risk. In Mary's case, she recently had been promoted to a position with broader organizational responsibilities and had needed support of all the major constituencies for that appointment. Therefore, the signals available to Mary in assessing her situation were not indicative of impending personal danger. However, a point to remember is that the organization was involved in consolidation activities, combining operations with other hospitals. A consolidation of services is a warning sign. Managers are placed at greater risk for not only job redesign but also political fallout. The tension involved in merging cultures and realigning priorities and programs within the organizations can result in power plays to assert control. In these situations, individual managers can become the target of aggression. Without additional information, it is not possible to determine whether Mary's situation could have been prevented or redirected to maintain her employment. It appears a judgment already had been made by her superiors that the situation could not be resolved.

Mary's reaction to the news is a common one. She was receiving unexpected news and experiencing significant personal loss. Her behavior is typical of someone in shock. Contacting her husband for support and assistance was an important first step in dealing with what had occurred and preparing the next steps. It should be noted that Mary did not make any major decisions that day and, in fact, decided to delay some actions until she had time to think things through. For example, although it was recommended in chapter 2 that the manager communicate what has happened to family, in Mary's case it probably was wise to delay that communication with her children until she felt composed and clear about what message to deliver. Discussing the situation in detail with her husband accomplished two things: (1) It gave her husband the information and allowed him to begin to process the news; and (2) it provided a source of significant support for Mary in the hours and days immediately following the event.

In this first journal entry, there are encouraging signs that Mary is making an effort to process what has happened and to be cautious about making decisions in an emotional state. It would have been preferable for Mary to maintain emotional control during the meeting with her superiors. However, given the nature of the news, her reaction is understandable. One tactic that Mary might have employed to avoid "sobbing uncontrollably" during the meeting would have been to stop the conference as soon as she understood its purpose and to request the meeting be rescheduled for the next day. If Mary's superiors agreed, this tactic would have allowed her time to deal with the shock of the situation and to compose herself before having to deal with details about her termination or specifics related to her transition.

Day 2

I am back in the office today, going through the paces of my job, doing my best to seem as though nothing has happened even though I feel as though my world is ending. It is good that there is much work to catch up on. However, I view the work differently now. I am sorting all requests and activities in my mind into categories— work I will complete, work I will reassign, and work I will never begin. I am beginning the process of letting go. But I must carefully cover any signs of this as no one knows what has happened. People who know me well are commenting that I seem different since my vacation. If they only knew!

My boss requested a meeting again today. He wanted to discuss any questions I might have about our meeting yesterday and to discuss next steps. I raised questions about the status of my employment agreement. I have an employment agreement for the position I held before my last promotion. An agreement for my new position is in draft form and has been under discussion and revision for several months. I wanted to know which agreement would be honored. Both address severance but differ in the degree of support provided. My boss said he would have to check on this and asked me if I have a preference about which agreement would be used. I committed to reviewing the differences in the agreements and letting him know. Given the uncertainty in this situation, I am uncomfortable not having an agreement relevant to my present position. I am having a difficult time trusting that things will just work out.

For now, there is no decision on when my resignation will be announced. I am to continue doing my job until this is determined. I am very careful to listen and document what I am told. I know the symptoms that people experience when they experience significant loss. I must be careful to ensure that I do not misunderstand information or forget important details. I decide to keep daily records in my pocket calendar, and, when additional detail is needed, in files.

I make it through the day. I called my husband several times today to just talk. He is the only person at home or work who has knowledge of this situation other than my superiors. I used my husband as a sounding board and as personal support whenever I needed it. This really helped me today, and we agreed I should continue as needed.

Commentary

Mary's journal entry, "I feel as though my world is ending," is very typical of comments made by individuals who experience job loss. Thankfully, these individuals soon realize that job loss, though extremely stressful, is not the end of the world. Being asked to remain in her position while waiting for the announcement of her departure only added to the stress of the situation. Mary was wise to keep busy with daily tasks and also to keep records of information on her termination. When emotions run high and circumstances of a departure are unclear, you should always keep a written account of conversations and events. Doing so should help avoid any confusion or miscommunication concerning those issues discussed.

Pursuing an equitable severance package also was a reasonable action on Mary's part. Even though she was technically without a contract, it would be in the best interest of the organization that Mary be fairly compensated in this situation. It is important to remember that you do not have to be a victim of the termination process; in many instances, you can be an active participant in defining it. However, this does point up the value of obtaining a written employment agreement that includes a severance agreement at the time of employment or promotion within the organization.

Probably the most important thing Mary did was to continue to seek emotional support from her husband. The most effective strategy for dealing with the seemingly overwhelming emotions associated with termination is to vent these thoughts and feelings with a trusted family member or friend. If Mary had been single, she could have sought the listening ear of a close friend or professional counselor. It is never healthy or productive to attempt to hold these difficult emotions inside. Eventually, they will surface and perhaps at an inopportune time.

Day 3

I woke up this morning and could not face another day of pretending that life is normal at home and at work. I reviewed my calendar and decided nothing that was scheduled was more relevant than taking time out for myself. I called my boss and told him that I would not be in the office today and why. He agreed and said he would notify my secretary that I would not be in the office today, I would be working at home and could be reached there if needed.

My husband and I took a long walk. He listened while I talked through the whole experience again and tried to put it into perspective. We had a long discussion about beginning my job search and the need to search nationally for a job. Since my employment agreement prohibits my working in the market for a year and since my salary is necessary to support our family, we agreed that we will pursue opportunities outside the area. It is likely that we will need to move out of state. I still cannot believe this has happened. We agreed again that this is not the time to communicate with our children about what has happened. Our daughter is preparing to leave for camp, and we don't want her away from home, dealing with her reaction to the news alone. We will continue to consider the appropriate time. I am happy for the delay as I am not strong enough yet to deal with other people's reactions, especially those of people who are directly affected by my termination. I somehow feel that I have let my family down, that I should have seen this coming and left the organization before it happened. And yet, I still cannot identify any information that would have warned me that I was in this kind of danger or that the decision could have been made so quickly. How did I go from being a high-performing, valued employee to an unemployed executive in such a short time?

I managed to fill today. I spent time with my children, worked on a watercolor, took extra time for exercise, and basically did whatever I wanted to—just for me. My husband and I made a commitment to walk in the early a.m. every day for exercise and an opportunity to talk privately about daily events. I think this will really help me.

My boss called late in the day to ask if I would be in the office tomorrow. I made a commitment to be there—to replace the mask and play the role as though nothing has happened.

Commentary

Many experts believe the best response to dealing with a termination is to leave the building until you can deal with the situation calmly. By staying home on day 3, Mary wisely acknowledged that she needed more time away from the organization in order to effectively cope with her emotional response to her termination. If you take the time necessary to deal with your emotions, you will be less likely to do or say something you could regret as you move forward with your career. The goal is for your transition out of the organization to be positive, regardless of the circumstances of the termination. Professional conduct during this time will always be beneficial to your future.

Mary's feelings that she had let her family down and should have seen her termination coming are common. Many who are terminated chastise themselves ruthlessly. Job loss is an experience in bereavement. The feelings of self-blame along with shock, sadness, anger, anxiety, and depression are all symptoms of the grieving and healing process. They are normal reactions that can be worked through and overcome. Mary made a good start toward working through these emotions by continuing to talk with her husband daily, as well as keeping busy with family, exercising, and participating in a hobby.

Day 4

Another normal (for the public) and abnormal (for me) day unfolded today. I was productive until my boss requested another meeting. He had asked me to research with a recruiter the average time executives remain in organizations in such situations. As we discussed my findings, he informed me that I might be asked to leave at any moment, and he would make no commitment as to timing. Yet, he still could not provide any prediction of when the announcement would be made. I was again instructed to continue with business as usual. I inquired again about the employment agreement, and he had no new information to share.

I experienced as much or more stress in reaction to this conversation as I had at our first meeting about this situation. I felt totally vulnerable, devalued, and out of control. I resolved to prepare for immediate departure in case this should occur. I think this was my way of maintaining some control. I did not want to experience what I have heard others describe—the degradation of having a security guard supervise you as you pack your belongings and then escort you off the property. I deserved better than that.

I called my husband. We agreed that it would be best if I came in that weekend and moved all but visible belongings from the office. Again, I would need to keep up the charade that all was normal. But I would secretly take action to protect myself from humiliation and from losing materials and belongings important to me. Although I did not relish the activity, I did feel in control of the situation and less victimized by taking action on my own behalf.

Commentary

Dealing with termination is a process that will not be completed in a day or two. Losing your job requires a grieving process very similar to that experienced after the loss of a loved one. This process requires time for acceptance and healing to occur. It was quite normal for Mary to experience a resurgence of negative feelings after her meeting with her boss. It also is typical to feel out of control, particularly in Mary's situation where the details of her termination were unknown. By resolving to prepare for an immediate departure, Mary took a positive step toward exerting control over at least a portion of her life. It also was prudent to remove personal materials from her office. Copies of successfully completed projects executed while employed in the organization, as well as personal belongings and any other nonproprietary materials accumulated while with the organization, should be removed.

Day 5

After the upsetting conversation yesterday, I decided the situation was entirely too uncertain. I made a call to my boss's superior to request a private meeting. I know I took a risk in doing this. However, I have great confidence in the personal integrity of this individual and believe that it is worth a try to see if I can get some answers. At a minimum, I want someone else in the hierarchy to know what questions I have raised and about my frustration in managing under these stressful circumstances. The delay in announcement and uncertainty about when I will be leaving the organization, when an announcement will be made, and the status of my employment agreement were my areas of concern.

The meeting went well. I felt really listened to and supported. I was given a commitment that the employment agreement would be finalized. I indicated a preference to proceed with the new agreement as it provided better transition support for me. I was told that although my boss may be unwilling at this point to agree to a time frame for the announcement and my departure from the organization, my last day would be 6–8 weeks from now. I would not be asked to leave at a moment's notice. It would be up to them to manage the situation. I also received a commitment that a decision would be made soon on when and how the announcement would be made. I felt better after the conversation. However, I decided to continue aggressively with my preparations for leaving the organization.

Commentary

Mary's decision to contact another superior in the organization involved some added risk; however, given the responses she had been receiving from her boss, it probably was advisable. Mary would be in the best position to judge the situation given her tenure in the organization and knowledge of both individuals from previous experiences with them. Although Mary perceived her boss as being unwilling to provide specific details, it may be that he was not in a position to do so. It is likely that others in the organization, including his superior, were involved in discussions and decisions about what actions to take. Based on the commitments Mary received, her strategy was effective in obtaining a better understanding of the intended time frame. She also was wise to clarify the specific reasons she had for requesting the meeting and what she hoped to accomplish. While it appears that Mary has made her own judgment about which of the employment agreements is preferable, it would have been advisable for her to seek the counsel of an attorney to ensure that her best interests are protected.

Week 2

There is still no decision on the timing of the announcement. It is very difficult for me to continue to convince people that all is okay as I do not seem myself, although I am trying with all my might to be so. I feel like someone really important to me just died, and I cannot tell anyone or let on that anything is wrong. Sometimes in meetings I just want to scream it out.

I continue to make steady progress on finishing work that must be done before I leave the organization. I am trying not to be obvious about not starting new work, so I continue to give the appearance that I am organizing new efforts. However, in my mind I have no intention of actually beginning the work. I know I cannot keep this secret much longer. This week I pressed for a date with no success, only a commitment that a decision will be made soon. The time must be right for the organization. But what about me? No one seems concerned about the effect this experience is having on me.

I have decided to shift my attention to job search activities. I will begin to contact people in my network and gradually shift to spending one-quarter to one-half of each day on job search activities. My resume and curriculum vitae are already up to date. Spending time on job search will allow me to focus on the future. I can no longer focus only on wrapping up work and maintaining a false facade.

Commentary

Mary's ability to hide her emotions and persuade people that all was well was understandably challenged after 2 weeks without a resignation announcement. She was most likely able to cope because of the emotional support of her spouse and her ability to keep busy with the details of the job. Being able to vent her emotions and do productive work will be vital to coping with her negative emotions, both now and during the job search process after she leaves the organization.

By shifting her focus to job search activities, Mary exhibited a very positive sign that she was coping successfully with her termination. The process of dealing with a termination is as individual as a person's emotions and will vary in length. At some point, however, you should see a change in your reactions. When you notice your thoughts are beginning to shift from what has happened to you to what you need to do next—from the past to the future—you are on the path to recovery. If this change had not occurred in Mary by the end of several weeks after her termination conference, it may have been necessary for her to seek professional guidance to help her cope with her emotions and move forward.

Week 4

The past two weeks have gone a little better than the first two. I feel more energized as a result of conversations with colleagues in the field and efforts to begin to identify job opportunities. I have made it through the questions that recruiters raise about why I would want to leave such a wonderful job. I talk about the consolidation and the stress that it puts on people in the organization, but I stop short of telling them that I have lost my job. The conversations seem to go well. I hope this gets easier as I come to terms with it myself.

I have finished most of my remaining work. All my office files have now been sorted and purged as necessary. A decision has been made that the announcement should go out in about a week, and I will leave the organization in about a month. Going public will make it easier to finish work and pass on projects. However, a new job will begin—helping the organization accept what has happened. I hope I am strong enough.

In networking calls, I visited with a colleague I have known for 15 years. These conversations have been very helpful to me, particularly during this time when I feel so isolated with the knowledge of my job loss. She listened to my latest update and offered support and this time some advice. As we move forward with the announcement, she cautioned me to not make it any harder for the organization, but to limit my efforts to make it easier. She advised me that my most important priority during this next phase was to take care of myself and to be sure to reserve adequate emotional energy for that purpose—not to use it all up in supporting others.

My husband and I are still looking for the right opportunity to tell our children what has happened before it is more broadly known and someone else tells them. However, we are sensitive to ensuring that all the children are at home together and well rested—timing is important.

Commentary

Again, Mary's renewed energy was a positive sign that she was prepared to move forward with her job search and her career. It also was a positive step to extend her support network to include a trusted colleague. Although spouses typically are able to provide emotional support, at times they too may feel traumatized by the situation and need relief. By having more than one support person to lean on, Mary provided her husband with time to cope with his own emotions and could even provide him with emotional support.

By networking, Mary was moving forward productively with her job search. Many people find jobs through word of mouth, and working the professional grapevine can provide a tremendous source of useful job information.

Week 5

We told our children today what happened 5 weeks ago in my life. I felt like I experienced it all over again, only worse this time. I would have done anything to avoid upsetting, scaring, or hurting them. I experienced a new level of helplessness as I watched them suffer over the news. The only thing I could do was be there for them. The uncertainty of our future was the most upsetting to them. Not knowing where we will work and live and when we will know was very difficult. We did our best to reassure them and to draw upon our faith. I experienced anew all the feelings of failure and guilt over this situation. I revisited in my mind what I could have done to prevent it from happening. Many of the feelings I thought I had moved beyond resurfaced. I became especially frightened about how I would deal with the situation at work in a few days when the announcement would be made and colleagues would react to the news. Would I have the strength to handle it?

As I expected, the announcement was not well received at work. People were caught off guard as there had not been any signs of trouble to warn them of this change. The announcement told of my resignation and plans to pursue other opportunities and was rather vague. People reacted in a variety of ways. Some assumed I had accepted a new position and congratulated me. Some expressed anger toward me for leaving the organization during such a vulnerable period. Others grieved over my departure and worried about their own future in the volatile environment of consolidation. I did my best to support others as I could but remained focused on surviving myself. This meant renewing my effort to stay on my exercise program, deciding to limit the hours I spent in the office to many fewer than normal, and continuing to devote increasing amounts of time to search activities.

Commentary

Although experts recommend telling children about a termination soon after it occurs, this must be a decision that each individual family feels is best. Mary and her husband determined the right time to tell their children based on their intimate knowledge of their needs. When the children are told, they should be allowed to express their feelings and be reassured that they will be taken care of. It is important to provide repeated reassurance and specific information in words that children can understand. If Mary's family had struggled with the situation, family counseling should have been obtained. The best protection against family stress is family cohesion, support, and communication. The family must spend time together, listen to one another, and make children feel a part of the team.

After the announcement of her resignation, Mary supported others but focused primarily on surviving herself. This is a necessary strategy when exiting an organization. Although professional conduct during your exit is advisable, you are not obligated to provide a counseling service to those who remain behind. You must concentrate on coping with your own emotions, obtaining equitable compensation, and moving on with your life.

Weeks 6 and 7

Since the announcement was made, people have continued to learn of it and react. I spend time every day either being stopped in the hall or receiving phone calls or E-mails from people who have just learned. It is emotionally draining for me to constantly be bombarded with people's reactions. I have purposely been visible and available. No matter what has happened in the organization, I still care about the people and do not want to isolate myself from them. I believe it helps them to see me going on with life. I may have lost my job, but I am not dead.

A lot of people have expressed support for me as I pursue other career opportunities. As they have approached me in one-on-one situations, I have determined those whom I feel most comfortable asking to serve as references. I have selected key individuals in the important constituency groups such as medical staff, executive staff, management staff, and staff nurses.

As time goes on, I am being left out of more meetings. Some people come to me requesting signatures and decisions, so it feels pretty schizophrenic to me. I am working hard to understand this is normal. My strategy is to do whatever I can to be helpful. I want to leave the organization on good terms.

I am continuing my job search efforts. I spend fully 4–5 hours a day now on this activity. It has helped me stay busy and feel productive. I have several active leads right now. I am getting better at explaining what has happened and am in control of my emotions most of the time. However, I can still be reduced to tears when people I have worked closely with are expressing their grief over the situation.

I am continuing my efforts to increase my general health and well-being. I have been exercising each day and as a result have lost weight. I recently changed my hair style and have purchased a new suit for interviews. Feeling fit and looking my best is helping to boost my confidence. Although I still feel victimized by what has happened, I do not want to look or behave as a victim. I trust that in time the feelings will abate. My focus is more and more external to the organization and on the future. I am getting anxious to leave the organization and to focus exclusively on building a future for myself.

I held several meetings with my boss to finalize the support I will receive in transition. Although I still do not have a signed agreement, I am assured I will have it before my last day. I will receive information soon about outplacement agencies available to assist me in transition. I have decided to work from my home office. Support that will be provided to me during my job search includes a computer, printer, office supplies, phone answering service at the hospital, and journals. I have held conversations with my superiors about what I can expect in the way of references. I am satisfied that I will receive good references and that they will be available as needed to support my job search.

Commentary

Mary's strategy to be visible and available in the organization is a good one. Although some of the contacts are difficult to handle emotionally, they provide an opportunity for both Mary and her colleagues to begin to work through the process of letting go, which will facilitate their ability to move on.

Mary is wise to identify and solicit key references while she is still in the organization. These references will be critical to her job search and eventual placement. Arranging for references would have been more time consuming and difficult to accomplish once she had left the organization.

It is normal in the last weeks of employment to experience transitional adjustments. Being asked to continue some activities such as routine approvals and decisions while reducing meeting involvement is symptomatic of the organization accomplishing needed work while beginning to transition responsibility to others within the organization. When the manager can cooperate and tolerate the stress of reduced involvement, it is helpful to the organization to have time to make these adjustments gradually. This minimizes disruption to the organization. Mary's strategy to be helpful in any way she can helps the organization and leaves a good impression.

As Mary continues her transition out of the organization, she needs to spend increasing amounts of time on job search activities. Efforts to improve her health and appearance are important steps in preparing herself physically and emotionally for the interview process. Most people who experience termination experience loss of self-esteem and self-confidence for some period of time. Yet, to compete for a job successfully, a person must be able to present well.

Another preparatory step Mary has taken is to assess her need for support during the transition and to negotiate for what she feels she has to have. When outplacement is offered, as in Mary's case, the support typically provided in an office setting is provided through the outplacement agency. Usually, the manager is assigned a small office to work from and given clerical support as needed. Some people need the structure of an office setting and routine to keep them focused on job search activities. However, this is a personal decision and should be based on the work habits and strengths of the individual. Mary preferred to work from a home office and so, instead, requested the support she would need.

Clarifying the type of reference that will be provided is critical. It is not unusual to worry about whether there were reasons for your termination that were not shared with you. As you pursue positions and near the final stages of consideration, you will need references from your most recent employer. You need to feel confident about the type of reference you will be given. It is also important to ensure that both you and your employer will offer the same explanation for your departure from the organization.

Week 8

Today was my last day in the organization. People were still requesting my signature—ironic. There was a reception given in my honor scheduled for 2 hours. However, it lasted 3 hours. Though it was tough to say good-bye to people I had worked with so long and cared about, it was great to see them one last time. There were lots of tears, and I am happy to say none of them were mine. That was my goal for the event—not to cry. The program was wonderful, I felt truly honored by the efforts people had put forth to bid me farewell.

Commentary

In a short 2 months, Mary has made great progress in accepting a significant loss. Although she will continue to cycle through feelings related to that loss for some time, her ability to continue to show concern for others and focus on her future are healthy signs of healing. Often executives decline to participate in a farewell reception, particularly when they have experienced an involuntary termination or when the organization chooses to have the executive leave immediately after the termination interview. When executive and organization can work amiably for some period, it is advantageous to the organization to provide a reception for the departing executive. It will likely be a difficult experience for the executive, but it enhances the ability of the executive and the people in the organization to move through the bereavement stages.

Month 3

I am enjoying my time at home. After exploring outplacement, which would have provided an office for my use, I confirmed my decision to use my home office. I know there will likely be a time of separation when I start a new job until we can sell our house and relocate the family, so I hope that being more available to them now will help us weather that part of the transition more successfully. There has to be some advantage to job loss—I have decided to make it advantageous to my children. They have always wanted me to be home more. Outplacement support is still available to me if I find this does not work.

My search activities now consume most of my day. It is amazing how much time it takes. I am now telling recruiters that I have left the organization and am involved in a full-time job search. I am comfortable with the message. Although I cannot work in this market during the transition per my employment contract, I have some consulting work to do for another organization outside the area. This has been a lifesaver for me. Work is such a huge part of my life that it has felt good to be able to work constructively on projects. Besides, the job search is such an emotional roller coaster as you wait to hear whether you will be invited in for interviews or how you compare to other candidates. On the whole, my job search is pretty discouraging so far. It seems I have been in search a long time, but colleagues remind me it has only been 6 weeks. The average search takes 6 months. My husband and I remind each other daily that we cannot become discouraged and must be patient. I vacillate between being glad that I am not working and worrying that I will never work again. Sometimes I fantasize about changing careers to avoid the risk of losing my job again for political reasons. But I end up reconfirming my interest in this work. I have decided that I need to get better organized as I continue my job search. It is hard to remember which recruiter goes with which opportunity, especially because there are often several involved in each opportunity. I am planning to set up a table to track my search activities. I will go back to the beginning of my search and include all the contacts I have made. This will also be a way for me to update my family on my efforts.

It seems strange to be cut off from the organization and people that used to consume 60–70 hours of my week. Only a few people keep in touch, and even then, the context for the relationship has changed. We used to talk about the work we had in common; now the discussion centers on my job search, and they are reluctant to discuss work. I wonder what people do in this situation when they have focused all their time on relationships at work? I am fortunate to have a close family and friends at church. My colleagues I have known and kept in touch with over the past 15 years have become increasingly important during this time as well.

Commentary

Every manager must evaluate his or her personal situation and determine what level of support will be required during the period of transition. Mary has anticipated that her new job will likely be outside the community and thus will require relocation. She has thought through the impact on her family and is taking the opportunity to do what she can to optimize the situation. A more structured environment is still available to her through outplacement if this does not work to her satisfaction. Generally, when outplacement support is provided, there is a collection of services available for either a period of time or up to a specific dollar amount. The most important thing for a manager to do is to be fully informed about what is available and then to make personal decisions about the use of this resource.

Mary's decision to communicate to recruiters that she is engaged in a full-time job search indicates that she has come to fully accept her job loss. It takes confidence and strength to be able to communicate this information, but in some ways it makes it easier for candidates because they no longer have to try to persuade people that they are employed.

Engaging in meaningful work either for pay or as a volunteer can be an important coping mechanism. Normally, managers and executives are accustomed to working long hours and obtain satisfaction from work accomplishment. When job loss occurs, a person can tolerate or even enjoy not working for a short period of time. Eventually, however, the time away from work can lead to depression. Finding activities that can temporarily provide meaning and purpose can be very helpful. It is important to ensure that these activities can be accomplished while still keeping the priority on job search activities.

Mary's description of the "emotional roller coaster" of job search is quite common. It is difficult to wait while the process proceeds at a snail's pace. It also is common to experience some difficulty in determining what types of positions you should be pursuing. This is particularly true if you are very experienced and have held a variety of positions. It is very important that you determine what your interests are and be persistent in pursuing opportunities that match. One way to cope with the frustration during this phase of job search is to develop specific measures for determining your progress. For example, setting goals such as sending out a certain number of resumes each week, making a certain number of contacts, recording calls received, and so on can give a sense of progress. The outcome of your search is a job, but progress must be measured in the steps you take toward that goal.

Mary's feelings about being cut off from the organization and the people she worked with are to be expected. Her ability to identify this as a concern indicates she is working through the loss. People who do not have family or friends outside the organization are at particular risk after unexpected job loss. This is especially true if their identity has been closely tied to their work. They may experience difficulty separating their personal identity from work identity. Usually, these individuals will require professional counseling and support.

Months 4–6

My search has continued. I have felt better after on-site interviews than earlier in the search process. I am able to get better information about the organization, assess strengths and weaknesses, and determine whether I can add value. I also enjoy getting feedback and meeting the people.

I am now in final negotiations for an executive position. The employer is agreeable on all points except severance. He does not see a need to include this in our agreement and feels that it may set a precedent for the organization or provide added risk. He is also not convinced that it is customary to address severance terms in an employment agreement. I discovered that he used a recruiting firm in the past that I also did some work with. I know their position on severance and employment agreements, so I have requested that he contact them for advice.

I have negotiated a start date for one month from now. I would like time to prepare my family for the transition separation and our eventual relocation. I also want time to prepare for my new role and some time just for me without the pressure of job search activities.

As I reflect on this experience, I believe I have done the best I could to respond to an unexpected event. I am happy to be employed again. However, I will never feel truly secure in a job again. I still believe competence is valued. I am proud of the work I did in my previous employment. I will endeavor to continue to put forth my best effort and to try not to worry about whether I will lose my job, but I will always stay prepared for a job search and will keep my network active and alive.

Commentary

Mary has progressed successfully through the stages of job loss and job search. Her strategy for finalizing the one remaining detail in her agreement, severance, should be effective. She is aware of the position the recruiting firm usually takes on this matter. By requesting that the employer make the contact, Mary has accomplished two things. First, she has placed the employer in the position of control, creating an opportunity for a win-win situation. He can obtain the information and act on it. Second, she has communicated that she is willing to trust the employer's judgment while making it clear that this is an important issue to her. She is taking some risk, but it is a measured one.

Delaying the start date is an important self-care strategy. In their eagerness to find a job, managers sometimes take the first one that comes along and return to work too quickly. After losing a job, it is doubly important to do all you can to ensure that your next job will be a good fit for you and the organization. It also is crucial to ensure that your frame of mind will allow you to focus on the new job. Taking time for yourself can abet the healing process.

Mary's reactions about job security are not unusual. Anyone who has experienced job loss often has difficulty believing the next job will be secure. Given the changes affecting the health care industry described in chapter 1, it is probably to Mary's advantage that she has shifted from thinking in terms of job security to taking personal responsibility for her employability.

Conclusion

On the whole, Mary did well in moving through the stages of job loss and successfully completing the job search process. Although she certainly has been affected by a significant loss, she has demonstrated significant coping skills. Her experience has offered us an opportunity to discuss management of involuntary termination. Although every situation is different, the principles applied in Mary's case can be applied in other situations as well. We do not always have choices about what happens to us, but we do have choices about how to react to those circumstances. Should you find yourself in an unexpected job loss situation, we hope that you can apply the principles described in this book and learn to be "in partnership with currents" you had not anticipated.